T0323918

Cambridge Elements

Elements in Religion and Monotheism
edited by
Paul K. Moser
Loyola University Chicago
Chad Meister
*Affiliate Scholar, Ansari Institute for Global Engagement with Religion,
University of Notre Dame*

MONOTHEISM AND PEACEBUILDING

John D Brewer
*Queen's University Belfast, Stellenbosch University
and Warwick University*

CAMBRIDGE
UNIVERSITY PRESS

Shaftesbury Road, Cambridge CB2 8EA, United Kingdom

One Liberty Plaza, 20th Floor, New York, NY 10006, USA

477 Williamstown Road, Port Melbourne, VIC 3207, Australia

314–321, 3rd Floor, Plot 3, Splendor Forum, Jasola District Centre, New Delhi – 110025, India

103 Penang Road, #05–06/07, Visioncrest Commercial, Singapore 238467

Cambridge University Press is part of Cambridge University Press & Assessment, a department of the University of Cambridge.

We share the University's mission to contribute to society through the pursuit of education, learning and research at the highest international levels of excellence.

www.cambridge.org
Information on this title: www.cambridge.org/9781009509671

DOI: 10.1017/9781009342681

© John D Brewer 2024

This publication is in copyright. Subject to statutory exception and to the provisions of relevant collective licensing agreements, no reproduction of any part may take place without the written permission of Cambridge University Press & Assessment.

When citing this work, please include a reference to the DOI 10.1017/9781009342681

First published 2024

A catalogue record for this publication is available from the British Library

ISBN 978-1-009-50967-1 Hardback
ISBN 978-1-009-34269-8 Paperback
ISSN 2631-3014 (online)
ISSN 2631-3006 (print)

Cambridge University Press & Assessment has no responsibility for the persistence or accuracy of URLs for external or third-party internet websites referred to in this publication and does not guarantee that any content on such websites is, or will remain, accurate or appropriate.

Monotheism and Peacebuilding

Elements in Religion and Monotheism

DOI: 10.1017/9781009342681
First published online: December 2024

John D Brewer
Queen's University Belfast, Stellenbosch University and Warwick University

Author for correspondence: John D Brewer, j.brewer@qub.ac.uk

Abstract: This Element addresses the opportunities and constraints operating on monotheistic peacebuilding, focusing on the three Abrahamic faiths, Christianity, Judaism, and Islam, which share a common origin. These opportunities and constraints are approached through what the volume calls 'the paradox of monotheism'. Monotheism is defined by belief in one omnipotent, benign, and loving God, but this God does not or cannot prevent violence, war, and conflict. Moreover, monotheism can actually promote conflict between the Abrahamic faiths, and with other world religions, giving us the puzzle of holy wars fought in God's name. The first section of the Element outlines the paradox of monotheism and its implications for monotheistic peacebuilding; the second section addresses the peacebuilding efforts of three Abrahamic monotheistic religions and the constraints that operate as a result of the paradox of monotheism. This paradox tends to limit monotheistic peacebuilding to inter-faith dialogue, which often does not go far enough.

Keywords: religious peacebuilding, peace, religious violence, monotheism, sacralised politics

© John D Brewer 2024

ISBNs: 9781009509671 (HB), 9781009342698 (PB), 9781009342681 (OC)
ISSNs: 2631-3014 (online), 2631-3006 (print)

Contents

1 The Paradox of Monotheism

1.1 What Is Religious Peacebuilding?

The British Victorian housekeeper and cook Mrs Beeton, who published perhaps the world's first cookbook, said about the recipe for hare pie, first catch the hare. This is good advice: start with the glaringly obvious. Namely, what is religious peacebuilding?

The phenomenon of religious peacebuilding is relatively new (on which for a selection see Brewer *et al.*, 2011; Coward and Smith, 2004; Mitchell *et al.*, 2022; Omer, 2020; Omer *et al.*, 2015; Schlack, 2009; Shore, 2009). There has always been value laid on peace within religious scriptures and traditions, but the process called religious peacebuilding emerged only in the 1990s. There are three ways of answering the question about what makes peacebuilding religious. Firstly, it is peacebuilding done to overcome religiously inspired violence and conflict, of which there is much around the world still (see Jerryson *et al.*, 2013; Murphy, 2011). Secondly, it can be seen as peacebuilding done by people with religious faith, and there are many of these too. Thirdly, it is peacebuilding that is motivated, shaped, and informed by the virtues and values that follow from religious doctrine.

The first is its weakest meaning, focusing on the kind of conflict to be pacified. All that makes it religious is the form of violence it addresses. The second describes some features of the people doing it, regardless of what it is they do. It does not specify what it is that their faith commitment brings to their peacebuilding, if anything. The third addresses the spiritual values, practices and virtues that inform what peacebuilders do. It is the strongest meaning to the term, for faith shapes the content, approach, practices, and form of their peacebuilding (on spirituality and religious peacebuilding see for example, Lederach, 2015). All three types will be referenced here in context, but attention is laid most on the second and third meanings of religious peacebuilding, where religious faith is central to peacebuilders and to peacebuilding.

There is another note about nomenclature as preliminary to this volume. Monotheist peacebuilding and religious peacebuilding are used here interchangeably. I am aware, however, that religious faiths and traditions outside the three Abrahamic monotheisms also value peace and engage in peacebuilding. Indeed, the honourable ambition to decolonise religion (on which for example see Omer, 2020; Vencatsamy, 2024), critiques the 'world religions paradigm' (which is not quite the same thing as monotheism) for its neglect of non-Western, non-white, and non-monotheistic religions, so the elision I make between religious and monotheist peacebuilding is technically incorrect. However, I persist with the interchange for two reasons. First, because there is no evidence that non-monotheist religions are any different in their ambivalence in practising violence while valorising peace despite not being monotheist. Second, because all the examples and references I make to religious peace-building here are to the Abrahamic monotheisms. In using them interchangeably, it does not mean that I am unaware of peacebuilding in other traditions (on religious peacebuilding in other religions see, for example, Blythe and Gamble, 2022; King, 2022; Mitchell *et al.*, 2022; Ngo *et al.*, 2015). Nor does it mean that I resist the decolonisation of religious studies; on the contrary, I favour it.

I want to begin, however, by highlighting the paradox of monotheism, for monotheist peacebuilding faces a problem derived from the very nature of monotheism.

1.2 The Paradox of Monotheism

To be monotheistic is to believe in one god and to deny the very existence of other gods. Indeed, God *is* one; not divisible, not reducible. While this is true of exclusive monotheism, which contends there is a singular God, even inclusive monotheism argues that the multiple extensions there are of God still derive from one true God, such as with the Christian Holy Trinity as multiple expressions of the one Deity. The oneness of God remains inviolate regardless of the kind of monotheism.

This oneness leads to further traits in monotheism. God is omnipotent, all-powerful, but also benign, loving, and merciful. God is thus personal, understanding the human spirit and human heart; after all, in Abrahamic forms of monotheism, humanity is made by God in God's image. God is not impersonal, distant and obscure; God knows us, since God formed us. God is made known to humanity and the benign and loving concern God has for humanity marks the Abrahamic monotheistic belief in the mercifulness and love that accompanies God's omnipotent power in the world. This is why God is symbolically represented and described as a parent. Love, patience, kindness, and mercifulness towards us are the principal qualities of God our Father (or Mother).

The doctrines and scriptures that adore this one God, which, although written by people, are portrayed as divinely inspired and inscribed, all value peace very highly. There are over 400 verses about peace in the Christian Bible, including the Old Testament, which is shared with Judaism, and Islam considers peace the most fundamental requirement of life; indeed, peace, the Qur'an, states, is found in the remembrance of Allah (see Mitchell *et al.*, 2022: 21–38). In the Christian tradition, Jesus, as the Son of God, is described as the Prince of Peace, and Jesus referred to peacemakers as especially blessed. Catholic social teaching, for example, considers peace to mean that people flourish and work to the common good, much as the Jewish idea of *shalom*, meaning wholeness and well-being.

The paradox of monotheism is that this all-powerful and loving God does not or cannot prevent war, conflict, and violence. This is true of the Abrahamic monotheisms and all other faiths and non-monotheist traditions, as the chapters in Jerryson, Juergensmeyer, and Kitts's (2013) *Oxford Handbook of Religion and Violence* attest (see also Murphy, 2011 for a similar edited collection on religion and violence).

Ironically, however, monotheism was born of violence and promotes it. Polytheist sects in biblical Israel and in the Islamic world had first to be defeated in military struggle in order for monotheist religion to dominate, including by both Mohammed as a warrior prophet, and by the Israelites under the command of Yahweh to smite the peoples of Canaan. Only the Jesus movement, growing out of monotheist Judaism, could emerge as fully monotheistic without the use of force. This has enabled Christian critics of Islam to idealise the life of Christ, comparing the militarism in the origins of monotheist Islam with Christ the lamb, whose only death Christ sanctioned was His own, although, as Johns (1992: 174) point out, this misunderstands the nature of Mohammed's militancy and neglects the violence done in Christ's name (see also Armstrong, 2007: 19). It also ignores the affinity between Islam, Christianity, and Judaism, with the Qur'an describing Christians and Jews as privileged 'people of the Book', who all share the one God's revelation to humankind through Abraham (Johns, 1992: 174–5).

With monotheism's origins in violence, it is not surprising therefore, that there are manifold religious wars and religious violence involving monotheist religions. Holy wars are those caused by or justified by religion, fought for religion against adherents of other religions, often to promote religion through forced conversion and territorial expansion. Notions of holy war exist in all three Abrahamic faiths (see Firestone, 2012; see also Firestone, 1996), and human history is replete with examples. Peace may be a religious virtue in monotheism, but it is not a religious practice. Markham (2022: 39–48), therefore, described two kinds of relationship between religion and peace, both of which permit violence. The 'pragmatic relationship' prefers peace to violence but accepts that peace sometimes requires the use of force, in what might be considered virtuous violence to eliminate, for example, human rights abuses and colonial usurpation. The 'oppositional relationship' Markham describes as one that opposes some aspects of peace, seeing justification in religious violence (on which see Clarke, 2014), using religious rhetoric and ritual to advocate force. This sees peace as acquiesce, submission, dissimulation, and what

Margalit (2010) refers to as 'messy compromises' that continue oppression, and should be opposed, even with force where necessary.

Perhaps a better way of describing the 'oppositional relationship' is not to say that some aspects of peace are opposed but that certain forms of peace are affirmed as preferable. The idea of virtuous religious violence finds its expression best in Lederach's notion of 'justpeace' (1999a), a new noun which makes peace and justice inseparable in principle (and in spelling). Peace and justice need to go together, and where justice is absent, a settled peace is unattainable, and the struggle for justice should continue. As a Mennonite, Lederach could never advocate violence, but he urges upon practitioners the need to identify wrongs and to put things right, although other scholars have connected the continued absence of justice as a threat to peace, a 'messy compromise' that Margalit sees as a reason for further resistance (2010). As Love (2022: 419) notes, religious violence has been some of the bloodiest, and the faith commitments of the protagonists did not prevent atrocious violence, leading her, and other people like Lederach, to rediscover 'justpeace' (which Love separates into two nouns as 'just peace'), the ethical grounding of which McCarthy (2022) locates explicitly in religion.

In this view, religion is both the ethical basis for justpeace and the justification for resistance where justice is absent. Thus, as Eisen (2011) argued, while peace is central to the Hebrew Bible, Jewish writers throughout history have embraced violence and accommodated themselves to it (see also Mitchell *et al.*, 2022: 31). The same is true of Christian and Islamic writers. The notion of the 'just war' is replete in Christian theology, in which the Bible is put to the service of the state in war. It can also be put to the service of God's chosen elect. The Book of Joshua, for example, is concerned with the violent holy wars Israelites engaged in to bring them to the land promised to Abraham by God.

As Bristol Baptist College's Centre for the Study of Bible and Violence therefore contends, there is a lot of violence *in* the Bible and a great deal more justified by it, to the point where the Bible can be weaponised and interpreted perniciously. As Helen Paynter, director of the centre, argues, 'the interpretation of Scripture matters. When it goes bad, lives are destroyed' (see www.csbvbristol.org.uk).

Moreover, religious violence entered a new and more destructive phase with the development of monotheism. Monotheism involves making and believing truth claims about the one God. The inherent tendency of each monotheistic faith to see itself as the one true religion, the font of all truth, can among some believers turn religious righteousness into self-righteousness. The point about self-righteousness is the conviction of the *un*truth of others. Violent religious extremism took on a new phase with monotheism precisely because monotheistic religion inevitably discriminates between the righteousness of the 'true believer' and the unrighteousness of the rest. Discrimination in belief and values can extend much further to result in 'unbelievers' being treated differently, facilitating the process which sociologists call 'othering', the drawing of boundaries around those considered an insider and an outsider. While these boundaries can remain solely moral, distinguishing between groups only by their different values and beliefs, the boundaries can also become social, political, and economic. In this case the religious 'other' is subjected to structural disadvantage and inequality and political disempowerment and oppression, which can provoke violent conflict between the groups who are religiously different.

Such systems of oppression are more likely to occur whenever religion and ethnic identity coincide, such that religion becomes associated with exclusive ethnic nationalism. In such circumstances religion can become wrapped up with both ethnic defence and ethnic expansionism, where religion is used by ethnic groups to defend their interests in a nationalist struggle of resistance or in nationalist expansion and colonialism. In these situations, combatants not only call on God to support the struggle, God is supposedly on their side. The often-cited quip about British colonial expropriation – that missionaries arrived with the Bible when Africans held the land, only for Africans to end holding the Bible and missionaries the land – is more than a funny aside; it is grounded in colonial reality. To understand the extent of this injury, Helen Paynter argues that scriptures might be approached by listening to the voices of those who have been harmed by the use of them.

Taken to extremes, the link between religion and nationalism can result in the elision of territory, identity, and religion (see Akenson, 1992) to give 'Chosen People' status to a religious group who become supposedly especially elected by God to inherit a land that is thought to be theirs by right of religious covenant. This after all is what the covenant with Abraham was all about. Afrikaners in South Africa, Jews in Israel, Protestants in Ulster, and the Pilgrim Fathers who colonised New England have all claimed chosen people status to give religious justification to their territorial usurpation. The Puritans who occupied New England, for example, saw their migration as a prelude to the last days and their colony was said to be the 'city on the hill' foreseen by Isaiah (Armstrong, 2007: 178). God's faithfulness to chosen peoples in this covenant depended on their faithfulness in occupying the land against resistance and in keeping themselves apart, especially from those who had previously held it. Loyalty to God is thus expressed through violent usurpation. The idea of a homeland in these circumstances is constructed and contested in part by means of religion.

Throughout history therefore, there have been many examples of religious extremism, now popularly called 'religious terrorism' (see Juergensmeyer, 2000). Religious extremism is very rarely conducted under a fairness rule that respects the human dignity of others and treats unbelievers as moral beings. Thus, holy wars are notoriously aggressive, abusive, and violent. These so-called 'moral wars' can be particularly morally degrading in the abuses they inflict on the human body of those who are the unelect. As Bob Dylan once penned in his anti-war song, you do not ask questions or count the dead with God on your side.

What I am calling the 'paradox of monotheism' therefore describes the dissonance and contradiction between the idea of one true God who is omnipotent and loving, all-powerful and kindly, yet who is unable to prevent war or dissuade believers from using violence in barbaric ways in His name. This paradox sets an intellectual challenge to the form and nature of God that many theologians and practitioners have taken up.

1.3 Reconciling a Benign All-Powerful God with Holy War

The challenge for theologians can be succinctly put. How do we reconcile the idea of an all-powerful loving God with religious conflict done in God's name and which God cannot prevent? It is possible to reconcile these by clever deconstruction of the terms of the debate, with scholars and practitioners unpacking variously the meaning of omnipotence, benevolence, violence, and religion. Through semantic deconstruction, it remains possible to see God as still benign, omnipotent and loving despite holy wars, but in ways that limit God's nature and form.

1.3.1

One form of reconciliation is to unravel the meaning of omnipotence. Some theologians refer to 'limited omnipotence' (see Brightman, 1940). Wrestling with the more general and enduring problem of evil rather than with the specific issue of holy war, Brightman argued that while God is good, omnipotence is limited by an incapacity to affect the very world that God has created. Hayes (1952) thus argued that Brightman saw God's will as finite. Many notable religious sceptics, such as David Hume, John Stuart Mill, and William James, also considered God as finite, with corners of creation where God does not, nor cannot reach, or comprehend. Brightman made a finer distinction, however. It is God's will, not God that is finite. God's will thus faces conditions in the world that are impervious to it, such as human sinfulness, people's free will and their non-rational consciousness, and 'natural evils' like floods, famines and earthquakes. Dilley (2000: 29–41) thus argued that God does the best that is possible against these evils; God does not choose to ignore such evil, some conditions are simply resistant to this will.

This is similar to Alfred North Whitehead's idea of 'process theism' as developed subsequently by theologians like Griffin and Cobb (1976; see also Griffin, 1991), in which God's will is limited to persuasion rather than imposed by coercion. Evils are thus a challenge not to the existence of God but to God's attributes. Griffin and Cobb (1976: 263) refer to the 'omnipotence fallacy', for God's will cannot be enforced by coercion. The tempestuous relationship of the Israelites with God chronicled in the Torah and the Talmud, despite their chosen people status under the Abrahamic covenant, clearly shows God was unwilling to control them through His coercive power. God is thus *not* omnipotent in the sense of being coercive in order to impose His will through force. God has a will for everything but not everything that occurs is God's will because of natural evils and the imperviousness of people to God's persuasion.

1.3.2

Another deconstruction is of the meaning of God's benevolence. There is sufficient doctrinal and scriptural support for the view of God as also vengeful and judgemental, breathing fire and brimstone. There is, for example, a lot of violence *in* the Christian Old Testament and the Jewish Torah. On this basis, God's love and mercifulness is matched by a discriminatory concern only for 'true' believers. Benevolence is therefore extended to those of the 'right' religion, not to all. This is a popular view amongst those practitioners and believers who use 'true' religion to draw boundaries in the social process of 'othering' in order to exclude outsiders (discussed further in Brewer and Teeney, 2015). Monotheistic religion is clearly wrapped up in the 'problem of large numbers', where cultural majorities have the ability to impose exclusion on minorities in the form of persecution, competition, or indifference. This is what we understand commonly by intolerance. Intolerance naturally leads to 'external othering', for religious majorities assert their religious differences in order to exclude minorities who do not 'belong'. External othering of religious minorities can show itself in religious persecution and violence, but most often neglect and indifference. Violent persecution is more likely to occur when the majority feels threatened and beleaguered, perhaps because of the size of the religious minorities, their political and cultural assertiveness, or links to powerful diasporas abroad, with indifference the likely result when the majority is a settled community and there is no sense of threat. It is a popular view in Northern Ireland, for example, that Protestants have participated in and supported violence against Catholics precisely because they are a beleaguered and precarious community (Dunlop, 1995) and are an 'unsettled people' (McKay, 2000).

It is in the context of this neglect and indifference that religion also gets wrapped up in what is popularly called today the 'problem of small numbers'. This concept describes the demand from small religious and cultural minorities for social, political, and economic recognition. We might call this 'self othering', for cultural differences are asserted by groups themselves to facilitate their recognition as a minority. This is not a demand that they become absorbed into the majority religion and made to feel they 'belong'; it is a demand for their religious difference to be accepted as a legitimate minority status. In this regard, cultural and religious minorities are asserting difference in order to better separate themselves. Sometimes this demand for religious and cultural separatism is pursued by violent means, deepening the association between religion and violence; on other occasions by political mobilisation.

Note that in the first case, othering is imposed on minorities from the outside, in the latter it is appropriated internally, hence, the terminology of 'external' and 'self othering'. In both cases, however, God's benevolence can be circumscribed according to religious differences.

1.3.3

Another way of reconciling God's benign attributes with the evidence of holy war is to deconstruct the meaning of violence to see some forms as religiously virtuous (on virtuous violence generally see Fiske and Rai, 2015). Theologians and philosophers have long discussed the circumstances in which wars can be just (see Atack, 2005; LiVecche and Biggar, 2022; Mitchell and Ray, 2021), and some 'true believers' contend that 'true religion' has to be extremist. For example, Christian monotheism was in conflict with Jewish monotheism in first-century Palestine over the universalism of Jesus's New Covenant, which extended the covenant to non-Jews. We glimpse the conflict over Jewish dietary laws and circumcision, for example, in the Book of Acts which discloses the violence directed toward Christians as a result, creating the first Christian martyrs through particularly grotesque deaths, although the monstrous deaths of martyrs were as much done by authorities in the Roman Empire as by Jews. What Armstrong (2007: 76–7) calls the thread of hatred throughout the New Testament against Jews was thus misplaced given the ultimate responsibility lay with the Roman imperialists.

Nonetheless, 'true religion' makes *in*tolerance rather than tolerance a virtue. For example, in the early modern period in Britain and its colonies, roughly the fifteenth to the eighteenth centuries, when religious conflicts were vivid and infused with empire expansionism and colonial expropriation, toleration was perceived pejoratively as a threat both to God and politics, since it reflected doubt in one's own religious truths and uncertainty in government. This is why zealots were able to conceive of executing dissidents within their own religion. Religious *in*tolerance was valued; religious tolerance was idolatrous. Some historians have referred to this as a kind of 'charitable hatred' (Walsham, 2006).

These examples are not restricted to first-century Palestine, the Crusades, or the wars of the Reformation and Counter Reformation, for Islamic State and contemporary forms of religious terrorism show them to be modern-day. This is referred to as 'pathological religion' (Appleby, 2012, 2015a), which is reminiscent of the ancient philosophical debate about the ethics of good and bad religion (on which see Orsi, 2022). The phrase 'toxic religion', meaning the same thing, has become popular amongst Christian practitioners (see Arterbon and Felton, 2001) and some theologians (see Morrow, 1998). In pathological religions there is no fairness rule operating to respect the human dignity of non-believers, who are morally enervated as a result. Dehumanising religious opponents in this way results in some of the most degrading brutalities inflicted on their bodies, which has witnessed the return of de-technological forms of warfare, such as the machete and the human suicide bomb.

Just war theory, nonetheless, legitimates violence, not, admittedly as a first choice, but as a moral necessity in the end. However, just war theory relates only to the conduct of states in conventional warfare, setting guidelines for what states should decide when entertaining the idea of war, and how they should subsequently conduct themselves during it. It therefore falls outside the moral purview of most forms of contemporary religious violence, which is mostly conducted by non-state actors.

Not surprisingly, the aftermath of wars often provokes consideration of the conduct of warfare. From the post–World War I Versailles Treaty (on which Love, 2022) to the post–World War II Geneva Convention, legal rules for the conduct of war have been established that are rooted in just war guidelines. Just war theory begins with the principle that taking human life is wrong but that it can become necessary for nation states to defend their citizens and to protect innocent life. The problem with just war theory, however, is that nation states routinely abrogate obligations under it, and are only selectively held to account for war crimes committed under international legislation. And just war theory only applies to nation states. It cannot be used to justify and give moral sanction to violence perpetrated by non-state actors or individuals. However, with the exception of a few theocratic states, such as Iran and Afghanistan under the Taliban, most religious violence perpetrated today is done by organised groups beneath the state to whom just war theory ought not to apply. Moreover, these theocratic states largely conduct violence against their own religious minorities and dissidents who support greater democratic freedoms, for which just war theory is again not appropriate.

1.3.4

Finally, some analysts reconcile an all-powerful loving God with the reality of holy war by questioning the meaning of religion when it comes to so-called 'religious' conflict. It is, after all, possible to tolerate 'true religion' when the limits of intolerance are defined by a fairness rule that ensures believers do not morally enervate others in order to deny their humanity. Religion is not inevitably extremist; the three Abrahamic faiths of Christianity, Judaism, and Islam give considerable doctrinal support to peace, justice, reconciliation, and tolerance. It is more often the case that extremists use religion for political purposes, giving their conflicts a religious hue even when the substance of the conflict is deeply political because 'true religion' so easily mobilises zealous adherents. Religious extremism is thus mostly a surrogate for political, social, and ethnic conflicts that are not disputes over religious texts, rituals, symbols, or practices. Religious violence is rarely about doctrine; religion occasions and facilitates the violence, it does not cause it.

The *Encyclopaedia of Wars* (Axelrod and Phillips, 2004: 1484–5) points out, for example, that out of the 1,763 known and recorded historical conflicts in its data base at that time, only 121 had religion as the principal cause, while White (2011: 544) gives religion as the primary cause of 11 of what he considered the world's deadliest atrocities. It is for this reason that Karen Armstrong (2014) refers to religious violence as a myth; what is mythological is not the violence but that it is religious in substance. Incidentally, the same can be said of racial violence; racism mobilises extremists whose conflicts are about other things.

In arguing thus, Karen Armstrong, a former Catholic nun who describes herself now as a freelance monotheist, confronts Richard Dawkins's argument in *The God Delusion* (2006) that religion alone has the capacity to motivate fanatical and violent bigotry. Condemnation of the barbarity of religiously motivated violence is a central feature of the 'new atheism', as it is called, but Armstrong contends that it is only with the modern period, and the rise of the secular nation state, that we have come to expect religion and politics to be separated; they were not hermetically sealed off from one another historically.

Since the Enlightenment however, philosophers have abhorred religious bigotry in favour of equality for all, advocating liberty, democracy, and secular values. In part, religious violence in the contemporary period in some theocratic societies is a resistance to such secularism, but it is also a surrogate for thoroughly political disputes that use religion to mobilise adherents.

Therefore, for example, anti-Muslim riots or attacks on Christian churches by exclusive Buddhist nationalists in modern Sri Lanka or by Hindu nationalists in India are not primarily forms of religious hostility but motivated by competition amongst market traders, fishermen, and farmers in Sri Lanka (see Brewer *et al.*, 2018: 156–9), and to promote an essentially political project in modern Indian through *Hindutva* (Hinduness) (see Anand, 2011). Poverty sometimes provokes the poor into very extreme forms of ethno-religious violence that are only superficially religious in substance.

Armstrong's argument, of course, is as much a straw person claim as Dawkins's, for no one argues that all violence is religious or that it is only religious violence that is barbaric; the history of genocide teaches us that lesson. Nevertheless, there is popular sympathy for the view that religious conflict is about politics not religion.

However, there are many examples where religious resources and symbols do define the conflict. Northern Ireland is one. Jonathan Swift, the well-known eighteenth-century satirist and Irishman, once said that Ireland had enough religion to make its citizens hate, but not enough to make them love one another. WB Yeats, another well-known literary Irishman, penned of the Irish that there is more substance in their enmities than in their love. It appears strange that a society noted in the distant past for the conversion of Europe, a land of Saints and scholars, and known today for maintaining very high levels of religiosity against the modern secular trend in the West (see Brewer, 2015), should be associated with enmity. This is no contradiction. Religion, while not the cause of conflict, is the social boundary marker that demarcates the groups between whom there is conflict, variously called Catholics-Republicans-Nationalists, and Protestants-Loyalists-Unionists. The conflict is over the legitimacy of the British state in Ireland and equal and fair access to its political, economic, and cultural resources for both Catholics and Protestants, but religious affiliation defines the boundaries of the groups who are in conflict, and for a very long time, patterns of inequality, structural disadvantage, social deprivation and political marginalisation cohered around religion to the disadvantage of Catholics. Likewise, it is difficult to deny the religious form to Islamic State's political violence, or that of Afrikaners in apartheid South Africa, when they invoked the Christian Bible to justify apartheid, or Israelis in the occupied settlements, where chosen people status ties them religiously and politically to a contested homeland supposedly granted by divine covenant in Talmudic times.

In these cases, the conflict is both political *and* religious, for religion maps onto and represents real material and political differences. The conflict is over the legitimacy of the state and access to its resources, but religious affiliation defines the boundaries of the groups who are in competition, religion provides some of the cultural resources for drawing moral boundaries between the ethnic groups in political competition, it facilitates ethnic and cultural 'othering', religious symbols become associated with political contestation, and faith-based organisations take sides in the war. Even if the religious affiliations of protagonists no longer have strong theological meaning for most people, cultural religion can survive as a relic of a former religious tradition despite changed political circumstances, giving a religious hue to the battle lines.

It is for this reason that some conflicts are *experienced* as religious in their form, even though the substance of the conflict is thoroughly political. This provokes debate in the academic literature about just how religious so-called religious conflicts really are (see for example, Gunning and Jackson, 2011; Taber *et al.*, 2023). Isaacs (2016) thus asks whether it is sacred violence or politically strategic faith. Academic disagreements about the extent to which Northern Ireland's conflict is religious also revolve around this confusion (for example, Barnes, 2005; Mitchell, 2006). The blurring of religion and politics in conflict is perhaps best represented in contemporary Israel-Palestine, where the political dispute over land is given a religious tone, with ancient Jewish religious texts used to justify the usurpation of Arab land, and the eschatology of the parties to the conflict fuelling various apocalyptic prophecies (see Freedman, 2019; Segell, 2023). To this mix must also be added the end-times thinking of US Christian conservative evangelicals, whose strong and unquestioning political support for the state of Israel is seen as a pre-requisite to the Second Coming of Christ.

1.4 The Distortion of Monotheism When It Is Politicised

We all know what happens to political conflict when it is given a religious colour, in terms of its dehumanising depravity in acts of war, its religious motivations and moral justifications, and the sacralisation of the perpetrators of violence, turning them into martyrs and heroes. Gentile and Mallett (2000) refer to this as the sacralisation of politics. 'Political religion', as Jones and Smith (2014) prefer to call it in their account of 'sacred violence', motivates, for example, both right- and left-wing social movements, and was a strong feature in the rise of various totalitarian states, especially fascism (see Gentile, 2006).

However, I want to ask a different question. What happens to monotheistic religion when it is associated with political conflict? Put another way, what happens to monotheism when we sacralise politics?

The answers to this question are important for they significantly limit monotheistic peacebuilding. Whenever politics, religion, and conflict elide, monotheism is mostly seen as part of the problem, implicated in violent contestation and the abuse of human rights; religion is not seen as part of the solution. I suggest eight negative things happen to monotheism when it is associated with sacralised political conflict:

1.4.1

There are hermeneutical issues that affect the interpretation of religious texts which weaponises Scripture. Doctrine is given a political interpretation, with politics shaping the canonical emphases. Human rights abuses – slavery, apartheid, sectarianism, anti-Catholicism, Islamophobia – have all been given Scriptural support in the past, and doctrine is readily invoked in encouragement of political actions. The Christian conservative evangelical support for Trump's authoritarian populism – amongst whom Trump is described as the New Messiah – is one example; the role of doctrine in motivating those who seek to limit women's reproductive rights in the United States today, or who resist gun control or who oppose transgender rights, are other examples. 'God, Guns and Trump' is a tragic example of the distortion of biblical hermeneutics under political religion, a very unholy trinity. Gorski and colleagues (2022) refer to this support as white Christian nationalism. Biblical hermeneutics allowed at the same time Afro-American slaves in the United States to see in the Book of Exodus their eventual liberation and the Klu Klux Klan to find justification for lynching them (Armstrong, 2007: 181). There is also doctrinal excision, where politically inexpedient texts are omitted from mention. In times of war, for example, the words of the gods of peace tend to be neglected. Loving thy neighbour and turning the other cheek are rather neglected themes in Christian pulpits during war. Hermeneutics can even affect hymnody, with hymn choice and worship songs reflecting political biases (see Whitnall, 2022, for a discursive analysis of some contemporary worship songs for their portrayal of 'the enemy'). The hymn 'I Vow to Thee My Country', written by Sir Cecil Spring Rice at the end of World War I in honour of his brother killed in the war, and sung to the very tuneful Jupiter from Holst's Planet suite, has some vicars in England banning it from being sung at weddings today, given its association with Remembrance Sunday and English patriotism. Given these connotations, it is thus ironic that Jupiter is actually described by Holst as the bringer of jollity. Venus is the bringer of peace, and Mars war.

1.4.2

Religious belief and practice are politicised. Religion is mobilised to provide the meaning, motive, and moral justification for political action, giving theological and scriptural bases to courses of political action. For example, scriptural support for anti-Catholicism formed part of political contestation in Ireland right up to the contemporary period (see Brewer and Higgins, 1998, 1999). Clerical support in Russia for the invasion of Ukraine is matched by clerical opposition to it in Ukraine's allies in the West, forming a good modern example of the binary of the just (and unjust) war. It was only with the first non-racial constitution in South Africa in 1994, and the election of the first majority rule government under President Nelson Mandela, that the Afrikaans Dutch Reform Church recanted their historic claim that Scripture upheld racial segregation; something supporters of slavery in the Deep South in the United States might follow.

1.4.3

The meaning of religion and religious identification are distorted. Religion becomes an expression of ethno-national identity, not an expression of faith. Faith commitment is wrapped up with political loyalty as a form of cultural religion rather than a demonstration of personal faith. Cultural religion and personal religiosity divide; cultural religion implicates an ethno-religious identity which carries no obligation to practice, so that religion becomes as much an expression of cultural and political identity as belief in God. It is the political and constitutional content of cultural religion that matters more to most Northern Irish Protestants, for example, than theology. 'We're not Christians, we are Protestants' is the absurd rallying cry of some Unionist protestors in Northern Ireland against Irish reunification.

1.4.4

Religion fragments. The chaos of political diversity affects the unity of religion as it fragments under denominational differences and doctrinal schisms, which can represent political differences as much as religious ones. The different political positions that evangelical churches in the Deep South of the United States take on Islam is a good example. Sunni and Shia differences within Islam reflect nation state allegiances as much as doctrinal disputes, pitting together the competing national interests of Iran and Saudi Arabia, for example. Differences within Judaism often map on to political differences in Israeli society, particularly over whether or not the protection of human rights is an ancient Talmudic principle, a dispute that is critical for the support some Jews give for Palestinian rights. The organisation Rabbis for Human Rights (on which see Brewer, 2010: 63–6), for example, argues that support for human rights is inherent in the Jewish Bible, and adopts a position on Jewish settlements in the West Bank that is opposite to the settler communities on the West Bank. Its support for displaced Palestinian communities often puts it in conflict with the Israeli state and its security forces.

1.4.5

Religion narrows in its form and nature in its search for religious and political authenticity. Fragmentation can cohere around narrower and ever more exclusive forms of religious belief and political position, with religious belief and behaviour becoming stricter, and the band of 'true believers' ever smaller. Liberalisation and secularisation have lost religion its monopoly of moral discourse, and fragmentation can result in very exclusive forms of faithfulness and 'truth'. This is reinforced when the religiously faithful retreat also into narrow political positions. The persistence of religious sects and cults in late modernity is as much for political reasons as matters of faith, and the political beliefs of sects separate them as much as does their religion, notably the commitment of Quakers to pacifism. The Protestant tradition in Christianity is particularly schismatic as a result of its principle of the priesthood of all believers and its historical support for the democratic practice of dissent in religion and politics, which results in continued church division and separation. In situations of political conflict, these religious schisms can get intensified to draw tighter boundaries around the 'true believers'. The Anglican Church is split globally over its response to sexuality and same-sex marriage, with resistance to liberalisation strongest in societies with ethnic and religious tensions with local Islamic communities, such as in North Africa and the Far East. The Irish Presbyterian Church has separated from its Scottish brethren over the latter's willingness to conduct same-sex marriages in church and is now even reconsidering its position on the ordination of women. The Northern Irish Boys Brigade, a largely Presbyterian boy's organisation similar to the scout movement, has separated from its Irish and British counterparts; from the former because the body wishes to resist any slippery slope to Irish reunification, and from the latter because of their perceived religious liberalisation.

1.4.6

In situations of religious plurality, where different 'true religions' offer competing versions of religious truth, religious diversity is difficult to manage through the usual strategy of the privatisation of religion, its separation from public life and retreat into the domestic sphere. In situations of religious plurality where, for political reasons, the elision between religion and culture is also strong and religious observance and identification remain high, it is almost impossible to promote the privatisation of religion. Equality of religious practice and belief is easier to enact in settings where religion does not matter, or not matter enough to want believers to have their beliefs count in public affairs. Cultural religion, however, politicises religion in the public sphere and makes religious plurality politically problematic. In such circumstances, monotheism returns as public religion (on which see Brewer, 2019). This has the effect of pushing religion back into the public square, despite secularisation and the decline in religious identification amongst the majority, giving political debates a religious edge and simultaneously witnessing the sacralisation of public space. Sacralised public space becomes a place for vituperative religious contestation, which can become violent. Cultural religion can, for example, proliferate hate crimes in public linked to religion, and encourage into the public square various groups normally hidden from it by their eccentricity but now emboldened under a religious impulse, whether they are white supremacists and their new-found evangelical zeal for Trump, Jihadists now encouraged to fundamentalist violence in shopping malls and pop concerts, or Jewish settlers on the West Bank dismantling Palestinian villages and homesteads. During the Protestant Reformation in Britain, for example, an odd selection of reformers were emboldened in the public square to even threaten the British king, ending up in beheading Charles I. The parading tradition of the Orange Order in Northern Ireland in celebration of Protestant King William's victory in the Battle of the Boyne in 1690 over Catholic King James, survives into the twenty-first century as a form of sacralisation of public space. In most areas they are welcome, but their marches are highly contentious in some Catholic areas where they are not wanted, but the insistence on their claim to a right to parade down the King's highway regardless is in part justified through religion. Countries that have avowedly secularised public space and public affairs are reeling under the attempts by various grassroots religious groups and far-right political extremists to sacralise it. France, Denmark, and Sweden, which support constitutional secularism, known as *Laicite* in France, have difficulty in recognising that their Muslim communities see the public burning of the Qur'an as sacrilege, and they fail to see that local Muslim communities are immensely offended to their religious core by cartoons that lampoon Allah. To local Muslims these acts are not just an expression of liberal, secular freedom of speech, but hate crimes. The equivalent in some Muslim countries is the violent repression of youthful demands in the public square for women's rights and for political democracy, which are seen by some governments as un-Islamic (on which see Sadeghi-Boroujerdi, 2023).

1.4.7

Religious spaces become divided and partisan: some religious spaces are out of bounds and are not seen as neutral and above the fray. Entering each other's religious spaces can become seen as 'roads leading to hell' and become particular targets by those asserting competing religious faiths and identities. Sunni and Shia extremists, for example, bomb each other's mosques. Sacred spaces that are shared often have a violent origin and can reflect religious controversies and contentions, becoming sites of vitriolic religious violence, such as the city of Jerusalem. It can be difficult to transform such sacred spaces into inclusive spaces of peace, what Kaldor calls 'zones of civility' (1999). This can limit the capacity for ecumenical and inter-faith dialogue, or at least force such dialogue into secular spaces, denuding it of some of its religious form. This is what happened in Northern Ireland, where inter-faith dialogue transformed into 'community relations' (see Power, 2007). What began as inter-church and inter-faith dialogue and exchange became secular and transformed into forms of community dialogue undertaken in secular, not sacred, spaces. With religion seen as part of the problem, and religious spaces not seen as neutral, religious peacebuilders tend to be forced into secret behind-the-scenes forms of peacebuilding. This was the problem faced by Christian churches in Northern Ireland's peace process (on which see Brewer *et al.*, 2011), where they were required to work in private back channels, leading many lay people in an uninformed public to subsequently disbelieve the churches played any role.

1.4.8

Finally, monotheism can become an obstacle to reconciliation, not a facilitator, seen as part of the problem, not part of the solution, with religiously motivated fear, anxiety, and hatred inhibiting and limiting the omnipotent God's benign capacity for love, reconciliation, and peace.

It is precisely this distortion of religion that results in what is described here as the paradox of monotheism with which I started: political conflicts corrupt monotheism when they overlap and elide with religion, identity, and territory. Because of this distortion, it is more difficult for monotheistic religion to be a site of reconciliation during and after conflict. This constrains and limits the potential for monotheistic peacebuilding.

2 Monotheistic Peacebuilding

As 'peoples of the Book' it is perhaps worth beginning a discussion of Abrahamic monotheist peacebuilding not with its constraints but with God's word. People's imperfect practice of God's teachings should not make us forget the power of peace in Abrahamic monotheism. In the three Abrahamic faiths, God's word comes down to us primarily through Scripture as divined through prophets and in the teachings of God's specially anointed on earth, that is, by His Son (Jesus) and divine leaders (Mohammed and Moses). Such scriptures speak loudly and with one voice about peace.

It is from this Word that the phenomenon of 'religious peacebuilding' emerged in the 1990s. While God's word is eternal, the reasons for the emergence of religious peacebuilding at that specific juncture, and the ambivalent reception it has received since, will be discussed shortly in Section 2.3, but any account of monotheist peacebuilding should open with God's unambiguous command in support of peace.

2.1 *Sola Scriptura:* Scripture First

'Scripture alone' (*sola scriptura*) began as an anti-Catholic mantra by Protestant reformers to criticise the influence of inherited Catholic Church teachings on Christian faith and practice, but it offers an insight into the marked disjuncture between doctrine and practice in monotheist religion. All three monotheist Abrahamic faiths give plentiful doctrinal support to love, peace, justice, reconciliation, and forgiveness, both as gifts that we can expect from God's benign parental love for humankind and as ordinary virtues which adherents should practice toward one another. The hermeneutical problem in pathological and toxic religion, previously mentioned, should not disguise that the three doctrines are fulsome in this support despite the manner in which some adherents use doctrine divisively. Christian monotheism, for example, is by nature reconciliatory since the very idea of the Holy Trinity is about reconciling the divine with human nature, with the new covenant empowered through Christ's death and resurrection being the way God reconciles with all humanity (rather than reconciliation in the Abrahamic covenant in Judaic monotheism only with an elect chosen people).

The three doctrines fulsomely espouse peace and non-violence. The Qur'an invites people to live a peaceful life, which reflects in the ubiquitous greeting in Arabic cultures of *salamun alaykum* which can be translated as 'peace'. Thus, the Iranian philosopher of religion Abbas Yazdani (2020) described peace as the primary principle of Islam, explaining imperfect practice as the result of poor teaching and wrong education, although the reasons why some Muslims support extremist violence are much more complex than this (see Fair and Patel, 2019). The Qur'an states that Allah invites us to the Home of Peace (10:25), with war and violence being an evil wrong (2:208). Allah 'loveth not aggressors' the

Qur'an states (2:190). The prophetic literature in the Old Testament and thus also in the Talmud, for further example, condemns violence, such as Isaiah (5:7), Jeremiah (6:7, 22:3), Ezekiel (28:16) and Amos (3:10). Even in the Book of Joshua that recounts the violent wars to establish Israelites' divine claims to Canaan, Joshua ends with a warning to Jews now to fulfil faithful observance of the Torah (Law) as revealed to Moses, of which thou shall not kill is a central theme. The Hebrew word *shalom*, meaning peace, wholesomeness, well-being, and everything that is implied in God's blessing and embrace for humanity (Nicosia, 2017: 9), appears more than 2,500 times in classical Jewish sources (Gopin, 2000: 77).

Similarly, the New Testament teaches non-violence, such as Mathew 5:38–9, Romans 12:17–21 and 1 Peter 3:9. As Wijesinghe and Brewer (2018: 138) argue, Jesus stood against the violence to which He was subjected – from Pharisees and from Roman authorities – by responding non-violently. This encouraged followers in the early church to portray Jesus as the suffering servant who embraces peace. Christian Scripture conceptualises the Christian life as a calling to selfless forgiveness, something dramatised every Lent in global Christianity through Passion Plays. Christ's death and resurrection centralise love, forgiveness, and mercy as principal practices in Christian monotheism, described best perhaps as vertical forgiveness, in that it comes down from God through Jesus to all humankind. Vertical forgiveness, however, acts as the foundational premise for what we might then call horizontal forgiveness, in which forgiven people are obliged thereafter to practice forgiveness in their relationships with others.

With respect to the practice of forgiveness amongst victims of violence in Sri Lanka's civil war, Wijesinghe and Brewer (2018: 151) contend that monotheist Christianity can all too often cast forgiveness as only a vertical relationship, going up and down between God and laity through the person of Jesus. During and after communal violence, however, it is important that forgiveness, mercy and love move horizontally between people themselves. This after all is why the primary prayer in Christian monotheism, the Lord's Prayer, couples our seeking of God's forgiveness with the rejoinder that we should forgive those who trespass against us. When it is horizontal, forgiveness informs human interaction and facilitates peace, love, tolerance, and compromise (Wijesinghe and Brewer, 2018: 152).

2.2 The Practice of Monotheist Peacebuilders

In contradiction to individual adherents who distort doctrine to justify and engage in violence, there are many individual religious leaders and laity in monotheistic religions who draw on religious resources, teachings, and doctrine in a peace mission. Three examples can suffice from across each of the Abrahamic faiths, in which in each instance, I isolate an individual as an exemplary case, Professor Mohammed Abu-Nimer (Islam), Professor Marc Gopin (Judaism), and myself, Professor John Brewer (Christianity). Whilst these are coincidentally all men, women peacebuilders are also mentioned, although we know less about them (on women peacebuilders see, for example Anderlini, 2007; Hayward, 2015; Hayward and Marshall, 2015), illustrating that many others could have been, and deserved to be, mentioned. However, I wanted to emphasise the individual faith believer's commitment to peacebuilding, and the religious resources they used to inform their practice, in order to illustrate religious peacebuilding in its two strongest senses. It is, however, only in part happenstance that they are men, for the invisibility of women peacebuilders ensures we know less about the faith commitments of women practitioner-scholars (see Hayward and Marshall, 2015 on the invisibility of women peacebuilders). They are particularly invisible when working outside the United States, such as in the Global South and in the British Commonwealth, as emphasised by the Commonwealth's Women Mediators Across the Commonwealth Network, whose Report was launched in conjunction with Conciliation Resources in April 2024 entitled *Personal Impact, Professional Resilience: The Psychosocial Implications of Peacebuilding for Women Mediators* (see htpps://c-r.org).

One last point needs to be stressed here. In outlining how these individual faith-based peacebuilders understand and outwork their religious motivation to peace-building, I blur the distinction between theology and social science and write by necessity in places as much as if I am a theologian not just a sociologist (elsewhere I have written on the opaque boundaries of the two disciplines, see Brewer, 2007).

2.2.1 Islam

Monotheistic religions are never hegemonic; Islam most certainly is not. While the Muslim religion penetrates Islamic culture, furnishing faith-based cultures to a much deeper extent than in other monotheistic religions, Islam is influenced by diverse national cultures around the Muslim world; variations in wealth, prosperity, and economic circumstances in different Muslim countries; local and regional differences in the demographic and ethnic landscapes in which it shares space with other world faiths and peoples; and the historical experiences and structural position of its adherents. There are also doctrinal differences that divide the various versions of Islam, securing contrasting interpretations of the Qur'an. These hermeneutical divergences, for example, sustain a faith-based Muslim feminism, despite the Western stereotypes of oppressed Muslim girls stoned to death in honour killings and veiled women dispossessed and silenced by male patriarchy (on Muslim feminism see Ahmad and Rae, 2022), showing that the Qur'an is replete with egalitarian principles and opposes the subjugation of women (see also Wadud, 2006). Doctrinal disagreements also permit an Islamic critique of fundamentalist Jihadist terrorism, denying its religious justification. For example, a six-hundred-page fatwa was issued in 2010 by Iman Tahir ul-Qadri, leader of the global umbrella movement of Muslim groups known as Minhaj-ul-Quran International, prohibiting on religious grounds any act of terrorism and banning suicide bombing without exception (see Kadayifci-Orellana, 2015: 440). The Taliban's interpretation of Islam in Afghanistan co-exists with that of the Organisation of Islamic Co-operation, for example, whose Mecca Al-Mukarramah Declaration in 2005 stated that Islamic civilisation is based on the ideals of dialogue, moderation, justice, righteousness, and tolerance, and that the Qur'an counteracts bigotry, isolationism, tyranny, and exclusivism (for these and other examples see Kadayifci-Orellana, 2015: 440). With nearly two billion adherents across different national cultures and societies, ethnic and linguistic groupings, and political and sociological systems, Islam cannot be monolithic.

Identifying an Islamic approach to peacebuilding might in the light of such differences appear mistaken, leading to accusations of selectivity that are the mirror reflection of the hermeneutical problems that sustain religious support for violence. Nonetheless, this is what Muslim scholars have attempted. One of the popular verses these scholars quote from the Qur'an is 13:11, 'God will not change the condition of a people until they change what is in themselves.' The Islamic faith thus predisposes human betterment and societal change. This upholds the idea of Islamic peacebuilding.

In an account of Islamic peacebuilding, Kadayifci-Orellana (2015) made the point that it is more individualised than in Western countries given the more limited development of civil society NGOs in Islamic culture, although such are not entirely absent. There are individuals, local leaders, and imams, doing charitable and humanitarian work, and mediating in instances of conflict on the ground (2015: 437). However, there are also umbrella organisations representing local Islamic bodies and communities who are agents of peace, whether in countries where Muslims are a minority or members of the majority religion. There is, for example, the Wajir Peace and Development Committee in Kenya, the Muslim-Christian Dialogue and Mediation Centre in Nigeria, the Peace Education Program in Indonesia, and the Islamic Red Crescent (on which see Benthall, 1997), to name just a few. As individuals and organisations, there are therefore many Muslims who practice Islamic principles of peace, drawing on

Islamic discourse and texts that try to transcend the differences inherent in Islam. After all, one of the very names for God in Islam, *As-Salaam,* makes reference to peace, a phrase which in Islamic tradition is said to date back to Adam, with the Qur'an advocating the spreading of *salaam* amongst people.

In identifying what is specifically Islamic about Muslim peace practices, Kadayifci-Orellana (2015: 443–5) mentioned the following principles:

- Peace is not merely the absence of war (conflict transformation), it is a positive affirmation to bring about social conditions (social transformation) in which social justice, economic fairness, political safety, and human security permits people to flourish and fulfil potential (see Brewer, 2022a: 24–7, for the distinction in the sociology of peace processes between conflict transformation and social transformation).
- Peace is an active not passive process, reflecting a life's vocation that involves continuous active engagement in peacebuilding (see Brewer, 2022a: 24 for the distinction between active and passive peace in the sociology of peace processes). Peace and justice cannot be achieved without an active and engaged community, without people who take responsibility for realising justice and peace as core Islamic values.
- Peace should realise harmony and balance in nature, society, and in human relations, in which regardless of diversity and differences, Muslims are enjoined to remember all people are made in the image of God and are thus sacred. Enemies should not be dehumanised.
- Justice is the key both to harmony and to establishing a sustainable and durable peace. It is the responsibility of all Muslims to work for the establishment of justice for all. This includes social and economic justice, and justice for all peoples, Muslim and non-Muslim, men and women.
- The values of forgiveness, love, and patience should dominate Islamic peacebuilding. The Qur'an enjoins people to be patient but not to be idle. Muslims need to work hard at forgiveness, love, and reconciliation, and not be depleted in their commitments to each when it takes time to achieve them.

As Kadayifci-Orellana realises (2015: 445), while these are Islamic values supported by the Qur'an, they are shared with the justpeace perspective of other traditions and religions.

The value of such work, however, does not lie in claiming their uniqueness to Islam, but in challenging orientalist assumptions that Islam is a warrior religion possessed by irrational, uncivilised, and barbaric adherents which so contrast with the rational, civilised, and peace-loving Westerners (on orientalist assumptions about Islam see Ghannoushi, 2011). As Mamdani (2002), argued, the so-called 'War on Terror' following the 2001 September 11 atrocity implied that

'Islam needed to be quarantined and the devil must be exorcised from it by a civil war between good Muslims and bad Muslims' (2002: 766). The thrust to the specification of Islamic peacebuilding is precisely to demonstrate its similarity to other monotheistic religions in making peace, justice, and reconciliation its central sacred values.

This provided much of the motivation to the pioneer of Islamic peacebuilding approaches, Professor Mohammed Abu-Nimer, from the American University in Washington, who served as director of its Peacebuilding and Development Institute between 1999 and 2013, and who founded the Salam Institute for Peace and Justice, as a research and practitioner-based body that focuses on intra-faith dialogue within Islam and inter-faith exchange between Muslims and other world faiths. What gives strength to his conviction that Islam is peace-loving is that he is an insider, Arab by birth and Muslim by faith.

His PhD work began with exploring the potential for conflict resolution between Arabs and Jews in Israel, graduating in 1993, and he has since broadened to the application of conflict resolution models to Muslim communities, leading to the advocacy of inter-faith dialogue between Muslims and other world religions, making him a scholar and practitioner in the model of John Paul Lederach, with whom he worked for a while in the Kroc Institute for International Peace Studies in the University of Notre Dame. His work on Islamic peacebuilding reflects in volumes like *Nonviolence and Peacebuilding in Islam* (2003), *Unity and Diversity: Inter-Faith Dialogue in the Middle East* (2007), written in conjunction with Amal Khoury and Emily Welty for the United States Institute of Peace, and *Peace Building by, between and beyond Muslims and Evangelical Christians* (2009), written with David Augsburger. The 2003 book was actually based on an earlier article in *The Journal of Law and Religion* in which Abu-Nimer first outlined a framework for how Islamic peacebuilding might be conceptualised (Abu-Nimer, 2001) that was expanded into the later publication. Both works appeared in the wake of the 9/11 atrocity, and the resulting hostile assessment of Islam, and he offered a view on the doctrinal support for non-violence in Islam and its potential for peacebuilding.

This backcloth was both an opportunity and a constraint. Public opinion was hostile to Islam and disbelieving about its peace-loving nature, but it also increased the interest amongst peace scholars and practitioners in the peacebuilding principles of Islam. Abu-Nimer became in great demand, as his professional and career development attests (see https://en.m.wikipedia.org/wiki.Mohammed_Abu-Nimer). His work involved, first, an exegetical analysis of key Islamic texts, most notably but not exclusively the Qur'an, and second, three case studies of conflict and peacebuilding in Arab history, including the first intifada in 1989.

There are two key foundations identified in the exegesis, the centrality of justice to Islam, repeating verses where all Muslims are obligated by God to remove injustice non-violently, and the importance of humanitarian action to effect human and social betterment for oneself and others. A whole series of virtues follow, such as respect for the dignity of all human beings and the sacredness of their lives as people made in the image of God, and an emphasis on equality, compassion, forgiveness, love, tolerance, and patience, all of which sustain the idea of Islamic peacebuilding (Ignatieff, 2017 would call them 'ordinary virtues' rather than Islamic ones). These virtues should be practised in relations with fellow Muslims, regardless of differences, and, most fundamentally, also toward non-Muslims.

2.2.2 Judaism

Professor Marc Gopin's work on Judaism and peace represents a fascinating entry into Jewish monotheism and peacebuilding. He shares some similarities with Abu-Nimer. He is a practitioner-scholar at the interface of theory and practice, with a biography that makes him both an insider to the Jewish faith, as an ordained Orthodox rabbi, and a marginal figure to the conservative religious mainstream and against the tide of hostile public religious stereotypes of Judaism by strongly advocating Judaism as a peace-loving religion. Gopin is the Director of the Center for World Religions, Diplomacy and Conflict Resolution at George Mason University in Arlington, Virginia. He was ordained in 1983 at Yeshiva University, a private Orthodox university in New York. The university is within the tradition known as Modern Jewish Orthodoxy that attempts to reconcile Jewish values and the observance of Jewish law with the requirements of living in the modern world. Jewish law is upheld at the same time as which believers should engage with modern life and culture in order to foster goodness, justice, and human and social betterment. Ultra-Orthodox Jews desire to keep modern influences out of their lives, seeing them as alien, but Modern Orthodox Judaism stands in opposition to this. Their notion of a faith-based life requires outreach to non-Jews and a commitment to co-operate with different traditions of Judaism, which includes, amongst many other things, support for giving women a larger role in Jewish worship, practical aid for the poor and disadvantaged, and a commitment to transform social and religious life to benefit the greater good. Not surprisingly, there is a strong commitment to justice in Modern Orthodox Judaism. They are not ultra-orthodox, nor conservative, but the obligation to the Torah and to faithful observance distinguishes them from liberal and non-practising Jews. In some ways, it is the epitome of North American East Coast Judaism, faith-based but shaped by wider secular liberal values.

Gopin thus lives and works within a thoroughly liberal culture in the Eastern seaboard of New England but as a practising Jew, Orthodox by ordination and inclination yet with core values that support the idea of Judaism as a religion of peace and justice. This, very importantly, requires engagement with all others who support the same commitment regardless of faith or non-belief (hence Gopin, 2015, has also urged the need for religious and secular peacebuilders to work together). This has made him pre-eminent both as a scholar of religious peacebuilding, where his work is concerned to identify Jewish principles of peacebuilding, and as a practitioner, where his praxis is devoted to improving relations between Jews and Arabs (see https://en.wikipedia.org/marc_gopin).

In several early works, Gopin championed the case for religion as a resource in peacebuilding (2000), especially in the Middle East, advocating holy peace as an antidote to holy war (see Gopin, 2002), and encouraging ordinary people to be 'citizen diplomats' when relations between governments have broken down (Gopin, 2009), which is a precursor to the new field of everyday life peacebuilding in the social sciences (Brewer *et al.*, 2018). However, it is the application of this work to peacebuilding in Judaism that is most relevant here. *Compassionate Judaism* was the title Gopin gave to his biography of Samuel David Luzzatto (Gopin, 2017), a nineteenth-century Italian Jewish scholar who had been the subject of Gopin's PhD and whom Gopin valued for his emphasis on inter-faith dialogue and the view that Judaism was a religion for humanity as a whole, without distinction or election, since human beings are all brothers (and sisters) in God's creation made in His image. Compassionate Judaism thus describes Gopin's view of Jewish monotheism as a whole.

Gopin's depiction of Jewish peacebuilding is best represented by his chapter on Judaism and peacebuilding in Coward and Smith's (2004) pioneering volume on religious peacebuilding, published in the wake of the 9/11 atrocity, which was amongst the first books to articulate the case for religion as a source of peace (see Gopin, 2004; but see also Gopin, 1994, 2003). Gopin's account is not about contemporary secular Israeli pro- and anti-peace politics, nor ultra-Orthodox religious resistance to Jewish peace movements, but the doctrinal support for Jewish notions of non-violence, justice, and peace. There are 613 *mitzvot* in Jewish texts as divinely ordered rules and commandments, given to Moses in the covenant and which Jews are obliged to follow since they are mandated by God. They give instructions about food, punishment, interpersonal relationships, and ways to worship, amongst many things, but some also cover key practices in peacebuilding. As befits a rabbi, his knowledge of these sources is comprehensive.

It is reasonable to summarise his argument about Jewish principles of peacemaking as follows:

1. Mourning is the basis for all Jewish conflict resolution. Victim communities can have abnormal levels of mourning that perpetuate over time, and the long history of suffering inflicted on Jewish communities worldwide requires religious peacemakers to confront and to utilise Jewish mourning.

    (i) Loss must be acknowledged so as not to fuel resentment and conflict.

    (ii) People should use Jewish mourning prayers to assist the slow and steady recovery from loss.

    (iii) They should engage in simultaneous co-present mourning and joint participation in mourning rituals, especially between Arabs and Jews, to transforms relationships by helping each group to mourn together what each has lost.

    (iv) Mourning rituals do not indulge memory but use mourning as part of peacemaking to help overcome hatred and suspicion of the outsider.

    (v) Mourning prayers and rituals in Judaism draw on unique Jewish values that promote shared values with other groups, including non-Orthodox Jews, secular Jews, Palestinians, and Muslims.

    (vi) These values constitute religious tasks – *mitzvot* – for faithful Jews, and include: involvement in the suffering of others; active responsibility for healing suffering; social justice and material redistribution and the sharing of resources to eliminate excessive inequality; and customs of civility as a religious duty.

2. Judaic peacebuilding is premised on the Jewish mandate to self-love, which in classical Judaism results in self-love extending outward to loving the neighbour as oneself.

    (i) Self-oriented love transforms into love of neighbour and the outsider because of the Jewish principle of *imitatio dei,* the requirement to imitate God.

    (ii) The ambition to be like God is psychologically empowering for the Jewish peacemaker.

    (iii) *Imitatio dei* obligates certain values in interpersonal relationships with the neighbour, as follows.

3. Jewish peacebuilding is premised on forms of personal relationships that are grounded in values that are biblical in origin and reinforced by faithful religious observance.

    (i) Jewish law and texts reinforce the importance of face-to-face encounters to address grievances.

    (ii) The principal expression of love is to find grace in the eyes of the strange other who is encountered, with the use of language that honours not humiliates them.

(iii) Saving the face of the encountered other is a key Jewish principle, a kind of moral gesture that reflects repentance and penance.

(iv) Honour and equality are at the core of Jewish law and must form the basis of any moral vision for a shared future between members of different Jewish traditions and between Jews and non-Jews.

4. Conflict mediation in Jewish peacebuilding is in the model of Aaron, the brother of Moses.

(i) It is a religious duty to mediate between adversaries to assuage hostility and empower healing.

(ii) Long-term empathetic engagement with the adversaries is essential for mediators, what today would be called 'shuttle diplomacy' (Nicosia, 2017: 10).

(iii) Mediators must show humility, even self-abnegation and the swallowing of a little pride, if it assists in conflict resolution.

(iv) Empathetic listening is a vital mediation skill.

(v) It is a Talmudic precept to help enemies when they are faltering with burdens, which helps in over-coming false and negative images of the enemy (see the tale of the overburdened donkey of one's enemy that requires assistance in Exodus 23:5).

(vi) Transforming relations with enemies is the key to conflict transformation.

5. The Jewish principle of *teshuva* is not limited to meaning repentance; it extends to 'returning' or 'turning around', which is the key idea to restoring broken relationships and healing from mistrust and polarisation.

(i) Turning relationships around should still involve restitution of the wrong, so that peace and justice coincide.

(ii) Turning relationships around also involves public expressions of regret, forgiveness and apology, and a commitment to change in the future.

(iii) Forgiveness without repentance is not biblical, for without repentance justice is diminished and history buried.

(iv) Conflict transformation requires the development of naturally occurring or manufactured cultural and physical spaces for the expression of remorse, regret, apology, and forgiveness.

(v) *Teshuva* must not, however, inject a sense of self-loathing in former aggressors but must occur according to a fairness rule that does not morally enervate the erstwhile enemy (on this fairness rule in the sociology of anger see Brewer, 2022a: 68–70).

It is interesting that Gopin concludes his account of Judaic peacebuilding by reassuring readers that he does not intend to impose it on society – and on other peacemakers we can assume – but to mobilise Jews who *are* religious to draw on religious principles in order to become their own peacemakers. The secular community and other faith traditions, he argues, can thus learn from their example.

With respect to Gopin's praxis, the best example for our purposes is his *Bridges across an Impossible Divide* (2012), which isolates a small sample of Jewish and Arab peacebuilders and addresses their 'inner lives', the experiences and biographical circumstances that have sustained their commitment to transcend this divide. This includes specifically their spiritual lives, as expressed by them in their own words in a rich ethnographic narrative. This shows us how some peacemakers who are religious have mobilised their faith to try to make a difference to an enduring conflict as an example to others.

The attention to peacemakers' spiritual lives reflects Gopin's whole approach to conflict resolution. It is one where peacebuilding requires both self-reflection, in order to examine introspective doubts and limitations, and motivation and drive, to rise above these doubts and to overcome such limitations (2012: 6–7). In his view, religion provides this combination of reflexivity and ambition. Consistent with his own faith tradition of Modern Jewish Orthodoxy, he argues that self-examination is not solipsistic but works only in conversations with others, in which together people confront and share their own tragedies, hopes, and fears (2012: 7). Knowing oneself is the way into knowing others. This is true for religion and for peacemaking. Thus, *Bridges across an Impossible Divide* does allow us to understand what it is about this group of Arab and Jewish peacemakers' religion that distinguishes them from co-religionists who support violence. Gopin suggests the following (2012: 183–5):

- They see their peacemaking as having some larger cosmic significance;
- There is a respect for the past combined with a conscious break with the past;
- They are focused on discovering new connections and relationships;
- There is a concern to cast a wide net of personal discovery and enlargement;
- Self-discovery facilitates their discovery of the other community;
- There is a commitment to hard work in dangerous circumstances to conquer fears;
- They embrace positive emotions and empathy toward the strange other.

Religion helps them overcome fear with love (2012: 185), a leap of love over an impossible boundary (2012: 198), which empowers them to resist manipulative religion and to love in difficult spaces of conflict (2012: 209). This makes them, as Gopin describes it, 'spiritual peacemakers' (2012: 209). This attention to the outworking of faith in the spiritual lives of peacemakers opens Gopin up to a new vocabulary and conceptual field, with affective notions like compassionate reason (2022) the heart (2016), and honour and shame (2003), which is reminiscent of Lederach's (2005) pioneering work on the moral imagination required for peacebuilding, all of which Brewer (2022a: 15–21) uses as examples of the re-enchantment of the vocabulary of the social sciences, which is a bedrock to the new intellectual space into which the sociology of peace processes must be slotted.

2.2.3 Christianity

Given that Christianity developed out of Judaism, and they share biblical texts, some of the principles in Judaic peacebuilding are naturally repeated in Christianity. Nicosia (2017: 14–16), drawing on Schreiter and colleagues (2010), summarised these as four practices, truth-telling, justice, forgiveness, and reconciliation. This rather under sells their prominence in Judaic and Christian peacebuilding. They are more than instrumental and efficacious transitional justice practices; they are like the four pillars of the Temple in which God resides in Judaism and which in Christianity are personified in the body of Christ as the living Temple. They are amongst the deepest faith commitments of Judaism and Christianity.

Such pillars are fundamental to these two monotheist religions, which thereby accords peacemaking to be similarly pivotal. Jesus is described as the corner stone or cap stone of Christianity (Ephesians 2:19–21, Peter 2:4–6), something Isaiah (28:16–17) pronounced as a feature of the Messiah in his anticipation of Jesus, and inasmuch as truth, justice, forgiveness, and reconciliation are personified in the body of Christ, peace is part of the cornerstone that upholds the whole edifice of the Christian faith. In being the cornerstone, Jesus is the foundation, the guide, the light, the promise of God to His creation; and peace becomes an essential part of this divine process.

The Christian Church lost sight of how peace is so focal to the whole Christian message, making much more reference to religious separateness, denominational schisms, and conflicts than peace, but peace is a cardinal part of Christian ethics, part of the very purpose that Christ as the son of God was given to realise on earth. Christian religious peacebuilders, therefore, have made much of the ethical responsibility of Christian believers to be especially blessed, as Jesus Himself described peacemakers.

The ethical obligation amongst Christians to be peacemakers expresses itself in at least two ways. The first is that a few internationally known conflict resolution experts bring a Christian faith allegiance to their work, similar to the faith commitments of the Muslim Abu-Nimer and Rabbi Marc Gopin. Christian faith commitments encourage their focus on general peacebuilding practices and, in some cases, their advocacy of religious peacebuilding. This faith commitment is mostly implicit but occasionally overt. In the United States there is the Mennonite John Paul Lederach, perhaps one of the world's foremost analysts of peacebuilding (for a selection of his work see 1995, 1997, 1999a, 1999b, 2002,2005, 2014; see Lederach, 2022 for his reflections on how his faith shaped his work), the Catholic Scott Appleby (for a selection of his work see 2000, 2012, 2015a, 2015b), the American Reform Church members Lee Smithey (for a selection of his work see 2011; Kurtz and Smithey, 2018) and David Little (for a selection of his work see 2007; see Twiss *et al.*, 2015, for a festschrift for David Little), and the American Dutch Reform Church member Nicholas Wolterstorff (for a selection of his relevant work see 1983, 2008, 2013, 2015). European examples might be the Presbyterians Gladys Ganiel (for a selection of her work see 2008, 2019, 2021) and John Brewer (for a selection of his work see 2003, 2010, 2022a).

The second way is the significant attention given to Christian activism, regardless of the writer's faith commitments. Thus, there have been studies of grassroots peacebuilding among Christian communities (Cejka and Bamat, 2003), and studies of denominational contributions, from Mennonites (for example, Sampson and Lederach, 2000), Catholics (for example, Schreiter *et al.*, 2010), the Redemptorist Catholic religious order (for example, Brewer, 2021a), Methodism (for example, Hughes, 2008), Quakers (for example, Valentine, 2013), Presbyterians (for example, Ganiel and Yohannis, 2019, 2022), and evangelical Protestants (for example, Ganiel, 2008), amongst others. There have been numerous studies of the interventions Christians have made in real situations of conflict as faith-based peacemakers, ranging from Catholic liberation theology in South America (for example, Chaves, 2015), conflict resolution in Zimbabwe (for example, Tarusarira, 2015), the anti-apartheid struggle in South Africa (for example, Shore, 2009; Taliep *et al.*, 2016), the Congo (for example, Arfani, 2019), Columbia (for example, Rios, 2015), Sri Lanka (for example, see Wijesinghe and Brewer, 2018), Ethiopia (Steen-Johnsen, 2017), and Northern Ireland (for example, Brewer *et al.*, 2011; Ganiel, 2021), to name only a few cases (see also the examples in Cejka and Bamat, 2003).

Christian activism in peacebuilding has isolated the role of key Christian leaders and other extraordinary individuals. These have been made in large international arenas, where the individuals concerned have global reputations, such as Archbishop Tutu in South Africa (for example, Allen, 2007) and the Rev Martin Luther King in the United States (for the latest, as an example, see Eig, 2023), or in local conflicts with people much less well known outside the region, such as in Northern Ireland with individuals like Fr Gerry Reynolds (for example, Ganiel, 2019), Rev Ken Newell (Wells, 2004) and Fr Alec Reid (McKeever, 2017), and in Sri Lanka with Fr Oswald Firth (Wijesinghe and Silva, 2021). Attention has also been played to the role of Christian women in peacebuilding, given that women's role in the Christian church has now been acknowledged and has expanded (for example, Hayward, 2015), which hitherto made them unseen, a point made by Hayward and Marshall (2015) for women with a variety of religious faiths. Bringing the role of religious women in peacebuilding into view, including those in religious orders, has, for example, allowed us to see for the first time their contribution to the peace process in Northern Ireland (for example, see Kirby, 2021).

The final illustration I want to make to highlight Christian contributions to peacebuilding on the ground is their role in transitional justice. Transitional justice is an area of peacebuilding that focuses on managing the legacy of violence as the peace process progresses and consolidates (see Turner, 2021). It includes policies and practices for dealing with memories of the past, a variety of victim issues, from material and symbolic reparations to trauma management, prisoner release and amnesties, the social reintegration of ex-combatants, issues of justice and the pursuit of crimes and human rights abuses, the forms and types of justice, from retributive to restorative justice, the various forms of truth recovery, from truth commissions and judicial enquiries to oral history projects, and the policies that need to be developed to protect human rights and prevent future abuses. This list is not comprehensive, but it describes many of the popular policies and practices for managing the legacy of conflict. Professor Daniel Philpott, Director of the Center for Civil and Human Rights at Notre Dame University, has championed religious contributions to transitional justice in several publications over a lifetime's career (for example, see 2006, 2007a, 2007b, 2009, 2012, 2015). Attention has been paid also to the role of religion in managing the traumatic aftereffects of mass atrocities (see Brudholm and Cushman, 2009; Rios, 2015), and some work has addressed the impact of ex-combatants' religion on their conduct of war and their subsequent engagement with peace processes (for ex-combatants in Northern Ireland, see Brewer *et al.*, 2013; more generally on ex-combatants and peace processes see Brewer and Wahidin, 2021). To this genre must be added the work of Christian theologians who have addressed key transitional justice processes like memory and dealing with the past (for example, Volf, 2006), the ethics of learning to live together after conflict (for example, Shriver, 1998), national healing (for example, Amstutz, 2004), the meaning and practice of forgiveness (for example, Torrance, 2006), and the elimination of sectarianism (for example, Liechty and Clegg, 2001).

The case study used to highlight Christian peacebuilding is the work undertaken by Professor John Brewer, and his research team of Dr Gareth Higgins and Dr Francis Teeney, from Queen's University Belfast. All are practising

Christians who lived and worked amidst Northern Ireland's conflict, born into to, raising, in Brewer's case, young children during it, having a close familiarity with the conflict that was enhanced by personal experience of living through it. Funded by the British Economic and Social Research Council between 2005 and 2007, their research focused on the role of the Christian churches in Northern Ireland's peace process (see Brewer *et al.*, 2010, 2011; Brewer and Teeney, 2015).

The Christian churches in Northern Ireland engaged in the following kinds of activity:

- Ecumenical activity (breaking down barriers, stereotypes and developing contact in a religious context).
- Mediation (involvement in local instances of conflict resolution and prevention).
- Cross-community and inter-church activities (entry into sacred and secular spaces to try to break down barriers).
- Involvement in wider secular peace initiatives (espousing peace and monitoring the conflict).
- Anti-sectarianism/anti-racism programmes (challenging the terms of the conflict and redefining it).
- Dealing with the problems of post-violence like trust-building and forgiveness (assisting with post-conflict adjustment).
- The churches as back channels of communication (provision of 'safe' private spaces for dialogue).
- Churches' participation in facilitating negotiations over political settlements and their iterations, and contributions to later selling the deals (the churches' public political role).

The Northern Ireland conflict, colloquially known as 'the Troubles', a term which seriously undervalues the scale of the deaths and injuries (one of the best studies of the conflict remains Ruane and Todd, 1996), gave us world-famous ecumenical communities like The Corrymeela Community (https://www.corrymeela.org) and The Cornerstone Community (https://www.cornerstoneni.com), but for a quarter-of-a-century, Christian faith-based peace activism in Northern Ireland was dominated by secret engagement between church figures and political and paramilitary leaders on the one hand, and by improving relations between Catholics and Protestants congregations on the other. Catholic and Protestants were encouraged to rethink their identity in less zero-sum terms, meaningful relationships were developed with political representations and paramilitary group leaders by clergy, like Rev Ken Newell (Presbyterian), Fr Gerry Reynolds (Catholic), Rev John Dunlop (Presbyterian), Rev Harold Good

(Methodist), and Archbishop Eames (Anglican), amongst many others, and there was continued witness by inter-church communities that stood as icons of what Christians tried to do to challenge the terms and ameliorate the consequences of the vicious conflict. To atheists like Richard Dawkins who claim that religion inevitably kills, we argued that while religion undoubtedly contributed to the conflict in Ireland, it is also certainly the case that without the churches the violence would have been worse. The motivations of the Christian peacebuilders never diminished over the thirty years of the conflict, despite no obvious success, but in the end, they made a meaningful contribution. What varied were the conditions that shaped the opportunities for Christian peacebuilding.

Premier among these conditions must be the spaces that were opened up for the churches as a result of developments in the wider peace process that provided opportunities for intervention, such as transitions towards a political strategy within the paramilitary organisations, the formation of a single military command in Loyalism with which to negotiate, the active interest of the Irish government in working with the British government in delivering their respective client groups, the improved good relations between the Irish and British governments, as well as the involvement of other international third parties, especially President Bill Clinton and Senator George Mitchell in the United States, the European Union, and leading South Africans who had earlier been prominent in negotiating the ending of apartheid. The back-channel dialogue that various religious peacemakers had established over the years with Loyalist and Republican paramilitaries, which were so suited to sacred spaces as places of secrecy, confidentiality, and anonymity, was able to be mobilised later to deliver support for the ceasefires and the eventual peace negotiations. Key religious figures orchestrated the manoeuvres with the Northern Irish political parties in combination with the respective governments, to help negotiate the ending of the violence.

The churches' long-standing contributions to social reconciliation were not irrelevant to this. The extensive development of ecumenist contacts between clergy, congregations, and denominations; the involvement of neighbourhood clergy in instances of local conflict mediation and dialogue; and the churches' participation in public peace initiatives and secular cross-community activities comprised the main activities by which societal healing and relationship building were attempted in Northern Ireland. This co-operation continued throughout the war. Religious peacemakers, however, could not proactively initiate these back-channel communications. They had to wait until the external conditions made the paramilitaries and the governments *want* to utilise sacred spaces for the purpose. This requirement was outside the churches' control, but when the time was right for the paramilitary organisations to talk to political parties and governments,

Christian peacebuilders' relationship-building made a difference (for a more extensive summary of the churches' role see Brewer *et al.*, 2011).

The problems these Christian peacebuilders faced, however, were twofold. The first was in being taken seriously in what was essentially a secular political peace process commanded over by professional peace resolution experts, and by political party leaders and government negotiators. It is notable, for example, that the churches in Northern Ireland, like the whole of civil society in the North of Ireland, were excluded from the final negotiations that led to the 1998 Good Friday Agreement. The second problem was the difficulty in having their contributions recognised by the public, who were largely oblivious to the secret back-channel dialogue the churches pioneered, or in having their efforts valued by lay people who had largely become anti-clerical in the years afterwards as a result of growing liberalisation, secularisation, and disaffection by the disclosure of church involvement in child abuse. This unholy trinity of liberalisation, secularisation, and disillusionment further encouraged the complaint that the Christian churches had not done enough toward peace in the North of Ireland, as admitted, for example, by the Anglican Archbishop of Armagh, the Most Rev John McDowell, speaking in October 2021 at a service in St Patrick's Cathedral in Armagh to mark the centenary of Ireland's partition (see https://churchtimes.co.uk/articles/2021/29-october/news/uk/we-didn't-do-enough-for-peace-says-archbishop-of-armagh).

Worse was the complaint that the churches had actually encouraged the continuance of sectarian division, in their institutional practices and structures and in their doctrines, making them as much part of the problem as part of the solution (see particularly Garrigan, 2010). The ambivalence of the Christian churches as institutions during the war, with their conflicting ethno-national interests and the political divisions within their own congregations, has persisted into the peace (on the Catholic Church see Scull, 2023). Appleby (2000) made ambivalence the central tenet of his analysis of religious peacebuilding, and it has not diminished since despite the fashion toward religious peacebuilding. This ambivalence is a wider problem affecting monotheistic peacebuilding generally and is central to any assessment of its strengths and weaknesses, issues to which we now turn.

2.3 The Rise, Fall, and Rise Again of Religious Peacebuilding

2.3.1 The Rise

The literature on religious peacebuilding emerged in the 1990s and has expanded rapidly since (for a selection see Abu-Nimer, 2013; Brewer *et al.*, 2011; Coward and Smith, 2004; Hadley, 2001; Johnston, 2003; Little, 2007;

Mitchell *et al.*, 2022; Omer *et al.*, 2015; Schlack, 2009; Shore, 2009; Smock, 2001, 2002, 2006, 2008). The academic and public attention given to centuries-long religious violence made people overlook the potential role of religion in peacebuilding. The shift in mindset, however, was very rapid. An intellectual space quickly developed in which researchers and practitioners began to advocate religious peacebuilding. This intellectual space had a circumscribed structural context that lay in the increase in religiously motivated violence in the Balkan wars and the rise of Islamic extremism in this period. The latter's 9/11 atrocity in 2001 brought holy war to the United States for the first time, and the Balkan wars in the wake of the collapse of communism, in Yugoslavia in particular, brought holy war back also to Europe in what had become a settled international order after the Second World War. The return of holy war was truly politically unsettling, arousing great concern at its reappearance, as marked in the debates between Karen Armstrong and Richard Dawkins discussed earlier about religion's capacity to kill.

The increasing importance of religion in post–Cold War conflicts, such as in the Middle East, the Balkans, and in South and South-East Asia, be this Afghanistan, Pakistan or India and Sri Lanka's civil riots, affected US foreign and domestic policy to the point where the focus on religion as a site for reconciliation became the reverse face of the attention on religion as a site of contestation. With the return of religious violence, the opposite side of religion's ambivalent Janus face came into view, with religion's capacity to heal and to transform. Religious peacebuilding thus found a stimulus.

A further part of this structural dynamic was the sense in which the United States was for a while the last superpower standing, thinking that with the collapse of communism and the end of the Cold War it was the police official to the world and could universalise and make hegemonic Western notions of liberal democracy to assuage global conflicts. US intervention in quasi-religious conflicts increased until the Obama and Trump presidencies, although only in a few cases like Somalia and Afghanistan was this intervention in military form; it was mostly cultural, diplomatic, material, and financial. As the sole police official to the world, there was a sudden need to understand the role of religion in conflict, in peace, in diplomacy, and in the provision of humanitarian aid, amongst other things. Religious peacebuilding thereby found another of its stimuli.

Much of the literature on religious peacebuilding, at least at the beginning, was from the United States because it is particularly suited as a cultural space for this kind of work. There is a plurality of religions in the United States as part of its racial and ethnic mix, but prior to the 9/11 atrocity, the country had never witnessed a holy war and thus had no historical folk memory of religious hatred and violence of the kind that affects most of Europe, which is steeped in folk memory of religious divisions. The US separation of church and state ensures no one religion has become the established faith and is accorded privileged political status. It is also a society where religious practice remains high, against the trend toward secularisation in Europe, which encourages people in the United States to take religion seriously. In the United States, where church and state are separated, there is an implicit requirement for public figures to articulate their private religious views in public, resulting in an easy penetration of the public sphere by politicians' private religious beliefs: religious enlightenment in the separation of church and state is taken to be the right *to* believe and for those beliefs to count in public affairs. In Europe, church and state are closer, with many state religions, and religious enlightenment is taken to be the right *not* to believe or to believe something entirely unorthodox. Religion is more privatised in Europe and politicians tend to keep their faith at home. As a result, the United States is a society in which religion is recognised as a rich resource in politics, part of political diplomacy (for example, Hoover and Johnston, 2012; Johnston, 2003, 2011; Johnston and Sampson, 1994), and foundational to domestic and foreign policy (see Bettiza, 2019). This is in sharp contrast to Europe.

The work of Johnston and Bettiza is worth isolating to illustrate the return of religion to US public affairs. Professor Douglas Johnston is the chief advocate of faith-based diplomacy and was founder and former president of the independent International Center for Religion and Diplomacy (on the current Center see https://icrd.org). He pioneered this approach in a co-edited volume with Cynthia Sampson as early as 1994 in their groundbreaking edited collection *Religion: The Missing Dimension in Statecraft* (1994). He went on to be an advocate of religious diplomacy in various academic roles, such as in the Harvard Kennedy School of Government and as Chief Operating Officer of the Washington-based Center for Strategic and International Studies, and in public service roles, with contributions as advisor to the White House, to the government, and to the US Navy. He was the inaugural recipient of the *Washington Time*'s Founding Spirit Award for Faith in 2007 and has been heavily involved in the National Prayer Breakfast initiative. He brings a deep Christian faith to his championing of faith-based diplomacy.

Gregorio Bettiza is British-educated and based at the University of Exeter. His first book was a comprehensive analysis of US foreign policy from the end of the Cold War to Trump (Bettiza, 2019). He argues that the interest in religion in US foreign affairs can be measured in four ways: a focus on advocating international religious freedoms as part of foreign policy, strategies for faith-based foreign aid, various interventions in

Muslim and Islamic politics, and positive engagements with religious stakeholders in multiple spheres around the world to understand the intersection of religion, violence and peace that defines much of the world's conflicts.

The repositioning of the research focus to address the need for faith-based policy interventions was sudden and dramatic. The United States Institute of Peace established a research programme on religious peacebuilding in the mid-1990s, which was prolific (see Smock, 2001, 2002, 2006, 2008), as did the Woodrow Wilson International Center for Scholars. The US Institute for Global Engagement established a 'religion and security' initiative in 2003 designed to explore the intersection between religion and political stability, and the independent not-for-profit Faith and Politics Institute was set up in 1991 in Washington DC (on which see https://www.faithandpolitics.org). New research centres and institutes sprang up to capture this zeitgeist, whose personnel have published the leading texts in this new intellectual field. Four can be mentioned for illustration in addition to the work of Johnston earlier. The Center for World Religions, Diplomacy and Conflict Resolution at George Mason University in Washington DC, is, as we have seen earlier, run by Rabbi Marc Gopin, who is an expert on the role that religion and culture play in conflict resolution, particularly in the Middle East (see notably Gopin, 2002, 2012). The International Peace and Conflict Reconciliation Program at the American University in Washington DC is led by Professor Mohammed Abu-Nimer, who, as noted earlier, is an international expert on inter-faith dialogue and Muslim contributions to conflict resolution (see notably Abu-Nimer, 2003) and who is also Director of the American University's Peacebuilding and Development Institute. The Yale Center for Faith and Culture (see https://www.faith.yale.ed) is directed by the theologian Professor Miroslav Volf, author of several pioneering works on faith, the problems of reconciliation following mass violence, and the role of religion in healing nations (Volf, 1996, 2006). Under Volf's leadership the Center focuses on what it describes as the key political question of the modern era: namely, what kind of society should we aspire to create? That is, social and cultural life, including peacebuilding, is thought of as political. The final exemplar is Brigham Young University's International Centre for Law and Religious Studies, founded in 2000 (see https://www.iclrs.org), to promote religious freedom across the globe and to facilitate the implementation of religious freedoms in the theory and practice of the law. Its location in Brigham Young University is no coincidence. The university was established by Brigham Young in 1875, a religious leader of the Church of Latter Day Saints, by which the University is still sponsored.

Religious peacebuilding thus grew rapidly at the interface of theory and practice, and it quickly developed sufficient credibility to sustain a new academic market of interest to theory-practitioners; not only in the manifold books cited here but also in journals. New journals began to appear in a time lag after a sufficient body of work on religion, politics and peacebuilding reached a critical mass. Examples are *The Review of Faith and International Affairs* in 2002, *Politics, Religion and Ideology* in 2000, Cambridge University Press's *Politics and Religion Journal* in 2007, and Manchester University's *Journal of Religion, Conflict and Peace* in 2007. The problem was that this group of faith-based religious peacebuilders was primarily a self-referencing academic community, whose works were popular amongst a public constituency whose faith made them responsive to religious peacebuilding.

2.3.2 The Fall

As we have deliberately stressed in the examples raised here, religious peacebuilding was widely advocated almost exclusively by theory-practitioners with a personal faith commitment, either located in faith-based settings or drawn into secular institutions, spaces, and programmes precisely because their faith was thought essential to facilitate understanding of religious peacebuilding. This was its strength. Religious peacebuilding had ardent sponsors and campaigners with an enthusiasm that reflected the certainty and conviction of their faith. And they were willing to practice religious peacebuilding, sometimes in the most dangerous and difficult settings, as part of the good works that emerge from this faith and its ethical values. However, it was also its major weakness. Religious peacebuilding confronted what Gopin (2015: 355) calls 'secular peace'. There are many dimensions to this clash: some are external, imposed on religious peacebuilding from the outside; others are internal to the way religious peacebuilding tended to be practised.

2.3.2.1 External

Chief amongst external factors behind the fall is the advance of secularisation in the West (as noted by advocates of religious peacebuilding such as Abu-Nimer, 2022: 562–4; Gopin, 2015: 356–7; Jakelić, 2015: 128), resulting in suspicion, and, at worst, hostility, toward religious peacemakers. The very governments, policy advisors, conflict resolution experts, and negotiators in the Global North, who deemed themselves specialists in peacebuilding and who tried to advance liberal democratic principles in their peacebuilding interventions in the Global South, where the peacebuilding measures were most needed, were resistant to religious interventions. Peace professionals, as they might be called, considered secularisation to be normative, in the sense of both being normal to society and a norm to the practised as part of the values of society. While the so-called 'liberal model of peace' (on which see Liden, 2021) had been discredited by the first decade of the new millennium by its sheer failure to bring an end to violence in the world's conflict zones and by its top-down approach that alienated local stakeholders by imposing Western liberal ideas of peace regardless of their local relevance or the local context (on these failures see Mac Ginty and Richmond, 2013; Richmond and Mac Ginty, 2014), all the subsequent variants and elaborations of the post-liberal model pre-supposed secularisation as normative in its two senses. As Liden (2021: 43) argues, alternative theories and models of peace did not go against the normative foundations of political liberalism, which assumed Enlightenment secularism and the declining influence of religion in the public sphere. Liberal and post-liberal models of peacebuilding are replete with ethical values – the elimination of harm, the promotion of the social good, social inclusion, halting of human rights abuses, and advancing distributive justice and humanitarian intervention – but religion did not provide their meaning or moral justification.

As sociologists of secularisation argued, God was dead (for a critique of the sociology of secularisation see Brewer, 2019). There is a decline in religious belief and practice, and the emptying pews mirror the diminished influence of religion in society. If it survives at all, according to sociologists, religion mutates into folk memory (Davie, 2000), turns into various forms of new age spirituality (for example see Altglass, 2014; Heelas, 1996; Heelas and Woodhead, 2004), or becomes privatised, restricted to the domestic sphere of the home not to count in the public square, permitting people to make gods of their own choosing, as Beck (2010) put it. Inasmuch as secularisation was the normative assumption implicit in peacebuilding, the peace professionals who practised peacemaking tended toward negative views of religion that helped shape dismissive attitudes toward religious peacebuilding.

Religion, after all, was part of the problem as they saw it; religiously motivated violence was the thing that required their professional peacebuilding expertise to quell. Peace professionals saw the deep irony of religious peacebuilders advocating non-violence when their faith traditions were themselves so violent. As we argued in Part 1 on the paradox of monotheism, the sacralisation of politics made religion politicised, distorting its peaceful message, turning monotheism in such cases violent, exclusionary, and militaristic. Monotheistic religions were involved in many of colonial and anti-colonial struggles, monotheism motivated religious extremist violence and religious terrorism, and much blood was spilled in the monotheist God's name in morally atrocious forms of violence inflicted on the innocent human body. Something that was part of the problem could not readily be accepted as part of the solution.

Religious leaders and institutions were themselves complicit in its fall. They often did not practice what they preached, had a penchant for using violence when it suited them to argue that God was on their side in a conflict, and key religious peacebuilding practices like forgiveness, mercy, grace, reconciliation, and compassion were, to hardnosed peace professionals, too nebulous and imprecise for operational application in real life conflicts on the ground. The monotheistic religions could not agree hermeneutically on the meaning of precepts like forgiveness, mercy and reconciliation, so peace practitioners devised their own operational definitions without recourse to Scripture (on reconciliation, for example, see Kelly, 2021). And the idea of prayer or meditation as peacebuilding practices was a step too far for secular peace professionals. Peace professionals therefore largely dismissed the efficacy of religious peacebuilding, denied its value even in cases where theory-practitioners advanced the contribution of religious activists in peacebuilding, and ignored any claims to its usefulness. Secularisation's spread throughout society further meant that the general public largely took similar views to the peace professionals, often denying any role for religious peacebuilding even where one existed. As Gopin (2015: 357) remarked, the potential for religion as a source of reconciliation, peacebuilding, and compromise, therefore, was unseen, and went ignored and untapped.

A final reason behind the fall is disciplinary closure by academic specialists in peacebuilding, which resulted in the exclusion of religious peacebuilding in the halls of learning outside this self-referencing academic community of faith-based religious peacebuilders. Disciplinary closure refers to the practices of academic subjects to draw boundaries in order to exclude other disciplines, thereby marking an intellectual field as their domain and expertise. It is part of the competitiveness that marks modern university life and runs counter to ideas about collaborative research (see Brewer, 2013). The salient issue here is that political science and international relations studies dominated the academic field of peacebuilding and defined it as their specialism. As I have written many times when advancing a sociological perspective on peace processes (for example Brewer, 2010, 2022a), disciplinary closure cuts off specialists from learning about the insights from other disciplines and subject areas. Lederach (2022: 63–4) made the point that with the dominance of political science and international relations studies in defining the field and approach to peacebuilding, these academic specialists also brought their Enlightenment secular practices in separating religion from their professional conduct. This had the effect of focusing attention away from religious peacebuilding or seeing it as secondary. Research specialists in religious peacebuilding who had personal faith, thus mostly underplayed it and kept it implicit (an exception is Lederach himself, see 2022: 67–9).

This opens up an intellectual space for an interesting and intriguing reflection about how academic specialists in religious peacebuilding with personal faith have faced opportunities and constraints in secular social science disciplines as a result of their religious beliefs, but regrettably here is not the place for such reflexivity. However, this question is relevant in two ways. Two consequences of this disciplinary closure are important to peacebuilding practitioners with personal religious faith. First, it promoted the expansion of the academic community of faith-based religious peacebuilders by drawing to it people who wanted their faith commitment to be expressed in religious vocabulary and amongst colleagues of like-minded faith believers, which was denied or supressed in the Enlightenment secularism of the social sciences. It is for this reason that the field of religious peacebuilding is disproportionately populated by people of faith, and why faith-believers working outside it in the professional social sciences mostly kept their faith implicit and privatised. It helped, of course, that some faith-based religious peacebuilders were located in universities with a strong religious culture, such as the Catholic University of Notre Dame. Secondly, however, it tended to reinforce the self-contained nature of the academic community of faith-based religious peacebuilders as a self-referencing circle. It is remarkable, for example, that Omer, Appleby, and Little's *Oxford Handbook of Religion, Conflict and Peacebuilding* (2015) has almost exclusively US-based authors. This contrasts markedly with the later cross-national volume by Mitchell and colleague (2022), such was the global spread of scholarship in the area, and the opening up to theory-practitioners from outside, making the circle less self-contained.

2.3.2.2 Internal

The very practice of religious peacebuilding was itself a weakness that contributed to its difficulties. In the United States, which for a long time was the primary site for advocacy of religious peacebuilding, the process is distinguished by three defining characteristics: (a) an emphasis on inter-faith dialogue as the primary form of religious peacebuilding; (b) the commensurate privileging of ecumenism as the chief peace strategy; and (c) eschewing comparative research in favour of the case study method. Methodologically, the single case study approach dominated. Single case studies got set alongside each other in endless edited collections and policy reports within this new literature, but there was no conceptual apparatus with which to compare the cases systematically.

The very titles of the pioneering books that championed the new literature emphasised the centrality of inter-faith dialogue, with examples like Gopin's *Bridges across an Impossible Divide* (2012); Smock's *Interfaith Dialogue and*

Peacebuilding (2002); and Abu-Nimer, Khoury, and Welty's *Unity and Diversity: Inter-Faith Dialogue in the Middle East* (2007). Peter Ochs (2015: 490) referred to this as 'hearth-to-hearth' dialogue with a third-party mediator, a description of close intimacy and familiarity in dialogue that he sought to advance. The problem with inter-faith dialogue as the principal peace strategy, however, was that religious leaders and followers by definition were unable to subdue their religious differences if they remained faithful to monotheist truth, being able merely to pursue their disagreements non-violently. It was difficult for ancient religious differences and folk memories of religious violence to be put aside. Fear, threat, suspicion, and ancient rivalries often clouded inter-faith dialogue and made ecumenism impossible to practice, or, at least, it hampered the potential for religious leaders to persuade more zealous followers of the value of inter-faith dialogue. Religious leaders matter to peacebuilding, as Sandal (2022: 552) unquestionably put it (see also Little, 2007), but the leaders of the 'religious other' are not usually perceived to be neutral and above the fray, and the task of taking more uncompromising followers along them with was a major problem in inter-faith dialogue.

Further, as Ochs (2015: 509) observed, the specific characteristics of religious conflicts can vary so widely that general prescriptions about inter-faith dialogue can miss the local dynamics. The nature or form of the dialogue needed to be sensitive to the local circumstances, requiring distance as much as familiarity, which religious leaders as insiders often failed to balance appropriately. Peace professionals saw themselves as outsiders, neutral and above the fray, and the 'local turn' in the liberal model (on which see Mac Ginty and Richmond, 2013) ensured that they drew on locals for the 'insider' knowledge and familiarity that they lacked. Inter-faith dialogue for them became secularised. As Marie Power (2007) termed it for Northern Ireland, ecumenism turned into community relations. Abu-Nimer (2022: 571), a chief theory-practitioner of religious peacebuilding, was thus forced to admit that the inter-religious peacebuilding that took place was not integrated, co-ordinated, or synchronised with secular peace professionals, governments, and policymakers. Religious actors were never reluctant to try to end violence, since faith was their motivation, but their efforts mostly occurred outside those of the professionals, who sometimes criticised well-meaning religious actors for making matters worse or getting in their way.

Another weakness in this literature is its concentration on positive cases, situations where religious bodies, para-church organisations, and faith-based NGOs did successfully bring warring factions together and where religion was above the fray and considered neutral, so that religious actors had genuine legitimacy as peacemakers. Women religious leaders have played an important role in this sense, as Hayward and Marshall's (2015) series of case studies demonstrate, and the many reports emanating from the United States Institute of Peace's religious peacebuilding research programme, edited by Smock (2001, 2002, 2006, 2008), focused precisely on cases where religion had made a difference to peace, although often only a temporary difference. Haynes (2009) isolates the successful cases of Mozambique, Nigeria, and Cambodia, where religion played a role, short-lived as it was in Nigeria (and short-lived also in Sudan, for Sudan see Cjeka and Bamat, 2003). Yet celebrate as we might the few – and often short-lived – cases where this outcome has occurred, we need a conceptual apparatus that focuses on the more numerous cases where religion is part of the problem and religious figures are not neutral, nor above the fray, but are integral to the conflict. It was precisely the perception of them as part of the problem that explains why, for example, the Christian churches were excluded from the negotiations that led to the 1998 Good Friday Agreement in Northern Ireland, along with all other civil society groups.

The reverse is as bad. Where theory-practitioners address these sorts of impossible divides, as Gopin (2012) described an unresolved conflict like Israel-Palestine, it discloses that inter-faith dialogue in such hard cases often fails, achieves little on its own, or plants seeds that grow so slowly as to suggest the ground is relatively infertile. For example, the success of Christian churches' back-channel dialogue in Northern Ireland, as we saw in this case study of Christian peacebuilding, only bore fruit when external conditions provided the right moment, circumstances which lay outside the control of the churches to dictate.

As I have written elsewhere (Brewer, 2022b: 525), religious peacebuilders are not on the whole professionally trained conflict mediators. There are some faith-based charities (for example, Christian Aid, and Trocaire) and humanitarian aid agencies with links to religious traditions (for example, the Red Cross and the Red Crescent Movement), with highly trained specialists, and some renowned conflict resolution experts, like John Paul Lederach, have a marked faith commitment, but theological training and ordination rarely equips journeying prelates, pastors, and priests with the skill set to know how or when to intervene in local conflict disputes, or to know what strategies to adopt to facilitate peacebuilding. This is why religious peacebuilding is largely reduced to inter-faith dialogue and ecumenism; they can better understand the need for communication with people of other faiths like themselves, and how to conduct it. Their role in conflict transformation is thus very limited.

However, religious peacebuilders are more skilled in what elsewhere I refer to as social transformation (on the distinction between conflict transformation and social transformation see Brewer, 2022a), the requirement to address the emotional legacy of conflict and promote societal healing, such as the practice of forgiveness, mercy, emotional empathy and reconciliation, and to introduce social justice, equality of opportunity, and fairness. These are areas of religious expertise. It is for this reason that religious peacebuilding comes into higher profile once the violence ends, and society emerges out of conflict to begin to learn how to live together in tolerance. The main contribution of the churches in South Africa, for example, came after politicians determined to abolish apartheid. The churches were active in the anti-apartheid movement, but they had no direct role in negotiating it away. Therefore, I argue that the input of religion into transitional justice is far greater than into conflict transformation alone (see Brewer, 2021b: 525–8). This argument is consistent with the life work of Daniel Philpott, who has long shown the many religious contributions to transitional justice (see for example, Philpott, 2006, 2007a, 2007b, 2009, 2012, 2015).

In order to properly locate the complex role of inter-faith dialogue and religion more generally in peacebuilding, and the manifold contributions of religious leaders, faith-based NGOs, and grassroots religious activists, three things are needed: (i) to focus on those problematic instances where religion is wrapped up in the conflict so that we can more sharply see the potential for religion to assist in reconciliation, tolerance, and co-existence; ii) to devise a theoretical framework that moves us beyond the case study method; and iii) to deploy this conceptual apparatus in cross-national comparative research of hard cases.

In the model I have developed, religious peacebuilding is much broader than inter-faith dialogue, and it identifies the wider sociological context that makes inter-faith dialogue meaningful or meaningless in degrees. This is not the place to repeat the model, for it has been explicated many times (see Brewer, 2010, 2021b, 2022b; Brewer *et al.*, 2010, 2011; Brewer and Teeney, 2015), but it is necessary to highlight here that what matters to the importance of inter-faith dialogue, and to religious peacebuilding generally, are key social processes.

These include the relationships religious actors have with the wider secular civil society and the state, the social spaces the churches occupy within the civil society-church-state matrix, as it was called, which we identified as intellectual spaces (as places for discussion of peace, development of visions for peace, ideas for conflict resolution, new ideas for reconciliation work, envisioning the new society, etc.), institutional spaces (religious organisations putting peace into practice in their own activities and behaviours), market spaces (their employment of social, symbolic, cultural, and material resources to actively support peace and peace work), and political spaces (their engagement with the political peace process, engagement with political groups and their armed wings, with governments, etc.). Another pivotal social process was the majority-minority status of religious actors, whether they were from the majority religion, a minority wing from within the majority, or were a minority religion from outside. The potential for key impacts on both the wider civil society and the state is shaped by religious actors' majority-minority status, as is explained further herein.

A final dimension to the model was the distinction between the social and political peace processes. This antinomy needs explanation (see Brewer, 2010, 2022a for fuller details). All too often peace processes are understood to describe the negotiation process that results in a settlement and the monitoring of conformity to the accord afterwards. We refer to this as the political peace process. However, the negotiated settlement is never the end of peacemaking, for accords mostly leave unresolved the processes for realising societal healing. By this we mean reconciliation between erstwhile protagonists, social relationship-rebuilding and repair across a communal divide, and the replacement of brokenness by the development (or restoration) of people's feelings of wholeness. These concerns are either ignored by negotiators in the political peace process or assumed to follow naturally from the signing of the agreement itself. The social peace process, however, fills this void and deals directly with societal healing. It constitutes an important dimension to peacemaking, going on well after the new political institutions resulting from the accord are bedded in. Religious actors have greatest expertise in social peace.

When analysed in these terms, it is important to note the opportunities and constraints that operate on churches and para-church organisations in entering the field of peacebuilding. The minority-majority status of the churches significantly affects the level of engagement and its forms, since majority religions tend to be established churches linked to the state or the religion of the dominant group culture. This majority status can limit their role in peace processes; a majority church can also be constrained in the critical positions it can take, and, broadly speaking, may be fearful of offending sectors of their congregations. Minority churches can be more critical, but also very vulnerable. One way in which the majority churches managed the problems of engagement, should events go wrong, was to restrict the involvement to 'unofficial' activity, although church decision-making processes and governance structures also made it very difficult to arrive quickly at an 'official' position. The distinction between 'official' and 'unofficial' peace work thus becomes another important element to the conceptualisation, for it helps churches manage the risks of public exposure both to themselves as institutions and to their members.

Church–state relations shape the kinds of peacemaking done by majority and minority churches, restricting the majority churches in the extent to which they can challenge majority community dominance and power relations. Church–state relations also make certain forms of minority church activity particularly vulnerable, whether these threats are real or imagined. The constraints imposed on majority and minority churches by church–state relations can be managed by different forms of official and unofficial intervention, allowing majority church peacemakers some autonomy when acting secretly and facilitating minority religious peacemakers, some of whom were in a double minority position and whose capacity for engagement required creativity in sidestepping official constraints. Churches mostly move officially quite late to develop policies for engagement, which is why unofficial forms of religious peacemaking can dominate as path-breaking activities during the worst of the violence.

2.3.3 Rise Again

Despite all the limitations of religious peacebuilding, its advocates have not demurred from acclaiming its significance in the aforementioned sorts of contexts and circumstances and with all the appropriate caveats. Notwithstanding the enthusiasm of the sociologists of secularisation, God is clearly *not* dead. Religion matters. Religion counts in the lives of billions of believers who retain a religious identity, and religion once again has public significance. With organised communal violence continuing, indeed growing as part of a particularly aggressive globalisation in those parts of the Global South where conflict predominates (see Brewer, 2022a: 18–19), religious contributions to its amelioration also endure. As I have noted elsewhere (Brewer, 2019), the return of religion to the public square and to a public role despite the obvious decline in religious observance and attendance in the West, is in part because of the relevance of religion to a whole series of global problems, including the reoccurrence of genocide to modern experience. Indeed, many of these global problems exacerbate conflict, including religious conflict, such as climate change, wealth disparities between the Global North and Global South, and health inequalities. Sociologists of secularisation are largely blind to the return of public religion, which is why its accounting is mostly done by sociologists from outside the subdiscipline of the sociology of religion.

As theory-practitioners of religious peacebuilding therefore argue, they need to move beyond the secularisation paradigm (for example Haynes, 2022: 475; Jakelić, 2015: 129) and to advocate assertively, as Ochs (2015: 494–5) puts it, that religion, while evidently being part of the problem, is also part of the solution. Ochs (2015: 498–501) contends that this requires theory-practitioners of religious peacebuilding to recognise that the complexity of regional conflicts necessitates strategic alliances between religious and non-religious peace-makers (which has encouraged Appleby, 2015b to refer to religious peace-building now as 'strategic peacebuilding'), the use of a variety of interests and resources in their peacebuilding, some of which lie outside of religion, and to 'move to the local' (2015b: 501) rather than impose solutions from above, attending to indigenous practices and vocabularies (2015b: 502; see Lederach, 2022: 77 on what he refers to as 'translocal' religious peacebuilding).

Abu-Nimer (2022: 563–5) therefore urges for better integration between religious peacebuilders and what here I have called peace professionals, examples of which he cites as the Finnish foreign ministry's collaboration with Finn Church Aid, the German government's Partnership for Religion and Sustainable Development, which brings together a collection of agencies alongside faith-based organisations working on the UN's Sustainable Development Goals, and the Faith Advisory Council to the UN Inter-Agency Task Force on Religion and Development, which advises on how UN agencies might engage with religious actors (on which see Karam, 2022). Gopin (2015: 367–8), another leading theory-practitioner, likewise counselled better integration of the values of liberal and post-liberal peace models and religion, particularly in adversaries being encouraged to feel the moral impulse to acknowledge responsibility for conflict and injustice and to seek repentance and forgiveness (2015: 368). In passing it is worth noting here a shift in nomenclature, with some advocates of religious peacebuilding moving language from 'peace' to 'development' in recognition that poverty provokes conflict, a move advocated incidentally by Pope Paul VI in an encyclical in 1967 (the shift is addressed by Appleby, 2015b; Karem, 2022).

Scott Appleby is relevant to any discussion of the future of religious peace-building. In a sense, the idea of religious peacebuilding began with Appleby, or, at least, was more widely popularised by him, and it is worth closing the discussion of its renewal with him. As the person primarily responsible for articulating the ambivalence of the sacred (2000), its capacity simultaneously for violence and peace, his defence of the theory and practice of religious peacebuilding (2022: 462–71) merits attention. Inter-religious divisions should not be denied or under-valued in a naïve and optimistic avowal of religious unity, he argues. Pluralism and diversity are part of modern life. Without saying as much, this is a warning to secular liberal and post-liberal peace professionals as much to Panglossian religious peacebuilders, for secular peace professionals too readily discount religious actors because they are divided amongst them-selves. Diversity of religious belief and practice is not the problem. Focus should fix on what Appleby described as the numerous historical and contem-porary ecumenical and inter-religious collaborations for forgiveness, healing, and peace (2022: 463). The persistence of religious ethics of compassion and reconciliation continues to motivate faith-based peacebuilding (2022: 467), and if diversity in religious belief and practice also persists, this is no more than a reflection of the ambivalence inherent in the human condition (2022: 470). It follows from Appleby's argument that liberal and post-liberal peace professionals need to take religious peacemaking more seriously (as Ochs, 2015: 503 also argued). And as for religious peacebuilders, Appleby says, they must continue to choose the good over more appalling options (2022: 470). Religious faith, one might say, permits them no other choice.

3 Conclusion: The Future of Monotheist Peacebuilding

Monotheism reflects the same ambivalence that Appleby says characterises the whole of humankind. Religious righteousness in monotheism can motivate peace and conflict; the paradox of monotheism is that it provides both opportunities and constraints on peacebuilding. We should not be surprised at this if ambivalence is so distinctive to late modernity. However, it seems unsatisfactory just to learn to live with ambivalence and to accept it, coming to terms with the contradictions between religion as a source of reconciliation, peace, and justice, and as a means to mobilise atrocious human rights abuses and killings. If we believe in a monotheist God of love, just accepting the frailty of the human condition seems inadequate as a religious response to that love. More is needed to reconcile us to God's love than learning to live with the ambivalence between peace and war, justice and abuse, and reconciliation and hatred. Faith should make us want to try to be better. Some thoughts on the future of monotheist peacebuilding thus seem warranted for someone like myself who takes seriously that I am made in God's image and that He loves me more deeply than any parent.

This is not the same question as the future of religion. The God of tomorrow is the same as the God of yesteryear. The religion of tomorrow, however, will be radically different from that of past times. While God is unchanging, our worship, devotion, and adoration of Him change constantly. Social change has always impacted on religion and its practice and forms, but not on God, who remains ageless, invariable, and unchanging. Whether or not religion lasts, and in what form, does not for a believer change the reality that God endures. Speculating on what the future of religion might be is thus secondary to the believer's faith that God will withstand religious change.

Yet it is important, at least for this believer, to try to improve the practice of monotheist peacebuilding so that it reflects God's eternal purpose as reflected in how He is revealed in Scripture. However much societies will reinvent gods and make gods of their own choosing in the future, the changeless monotheist God in which I believe wants humankind to aspire to better things, and that means in this instance, overcoming ambivalence by aspiring to improve religious peacebuilding. I therefore want to conclude with two suggestions: the first aimed at professional peacebuilders, the second at religious believers in the three Abrahamic monotheisms.

3.1 Peace Professionals

Governments, policy analysts, conflict resolution experts, and trained mediators need self-reflection as much as Gopin (2012) says religious peacebuilders do, in order to locate their professional objections to religious peacebuilding in a secularisation paradigm that is socially constructed rather than absolute and is just as much a matter of personal belief as is religious peacebuilders' faith. They have no more a handle on the future of religion as does the religious believer. The paradigmatic assumption that it will wither is less grounded in fact than the precipitous increase in belief. 'The secularising West and the rapidly growing rest' is a quip that should at least make peace professional take religion and religious peacebuilding seriously. Better knowledge is therefore required about the three Abrahamic monotheisms to see their doctrinal respect for tolerance, civility, peace, and reconciliation. Ignorance of these traditions needs to be replaced with the awareness that these religious virtues offer opportunities that can be used in secular peacebuilding efforts and strategies, and which furnish religious actors who hold them with virtues that make them capable of helping peace professionals to make a difference. Toxic and pathological religion is not the whole of religion. Peace professionals therefore should always consider the extent to which religious leaders, faith-based NGOs, and local grassroots religious actors can be involved in conflict resolution and peacebuilding. This may require conflict resolution training for peace professionals to include curriculum on religious literacy and sensitivity. It also seems particularly important for peace professionals to seek out and encourage the contribution of religious women and non-Western women religious actors, such as the Women Mediators Across the Commonwealth Network and Conciliation Resources (on the latter see https://c-r.org).

3.2 Religious Peacebuilders

Toxic and pathological religion distorts God's word. People of faith interested in peacebuilding need to return to God's message as revealed in Scripture. This means they must lead a counter-narrative that emphasises, as Armstrong (2014: 224) phrases it, charity, kindness, love, and peace. The power of God's word needs to be rescued from the toxic and pathological manipulators in order to make the principal Scriptural interpretation one of love, respect, and tolerance. Ordination and training for religious leaders in all three Abrahamic faiths should therefore be interrogated for any implicit or explicit gestures towards toxicity and pathology. Open condemnation should be aimed at those who use Scripture to exploit, demean, dehumanise, and morally enervate others, including those within their own tradition as well as across the different Abrahamic monotheisms.

Religious peacebuilders need to practice virtue in their own lives. This means that religious institutions, faith-based and para-church organisations, and religious leaders need to be reflexive in ensuring that they live up to God's command to love. In Scripture, peace, tolerance, and reconciliation follow on from and emerge out of love. The US theologian and philosopher Nicholas Wolterstorff in his early work elided together justice and peace, although not as a single noun (see Wolterstorff, 1983) in the mould that Lederach does now, an idea which runs like a purple thread through Omer, Appleby, and Little's (2015) *Oxford Handbook of Religion, Conflict and Peacebuilding*. In his later work however, Wolterstorff proposed 'justice-love' as a new noun (see Wolterstorff, 2015). Wolterstorff refers to this as 'care agapism', agape being the Greek word for love as translated in the New Testament. That is, care for others becomes a signal measure of love, both of God's love for us and in our practice as His followers to love others. This is the principal tenet of all three Abrahamic monotheisms. Monotheism can be defined by its emphasis on God as benign, loving, kindly, merciful, and forgiving. While human frailty distorts this, monotheist peacebuilding must live up to this tough command to love others. For our monotheist God in the Abrahamic tradition, love is reciprocal. God is love, and to love God, we must love others. This is true of all Abrahamic monotheisms. Tough, indeed – but faith is not easy.

Religious unity across the Abrahamic monotheisms is an unrealistic goal for inter-faith dialogue and inter-faith peacebuilding. Religious peacebuilders better serve the cause of peace by remaining solidly within their own tradition, earning legitimacy as representatives of it, while encouraging their faith tradition to reach out to others on the basis of respect, tolerance, peace, and love toward people of other traditions. This outreach in love should be to those within their own tradition who show toxicity and pathology in their interpretation of texts and to people of other traditions, whether monotheist or not.

Religious peacebuilders need to acquire resilience when they encounter dangerous and intimidating situations from within their own community under accusations of profanity, deviation, and sacrilege, and to seek exegetical support from Scripture to uphold their charitable interpretations of text.

Strategic alliances should be developed with others who share such charitable-ness, as well as from secular peace professionals. Religious peacebuilders thus need to develop prophetic leadership in being ahead of their community and taking them forward, as well as garnering a prophetic presence on the ground in working alongside people affected by the violence and sharing their pain and victimhood. What elsewhere I called 'rubber-band leadership' (Brewer *et al.*, 2011), in which leaders permit themselves to be pulled back by followers by not wanting to be too far ahead of them, is not prophetic leadership. Prophetic leadership displays courage, resilience, and perseverance in doing what doctrine reveals as the right thing. Prophetic leadership does what is right as revealed in Scripture, not what followers permit as being acceptable.

The quality of God as revealed through Scripture is an embracing, all-encompassing, and inclusive love, but the practice of religion marginalises some categories of people, such as women, LGBTQ people, migrants, the young and the elderly, and, in some societies, people of colour and members of ethnic minorities. Faith, however, is not the preserve of people only like ourselves; nor should be faith-based peacebuilding. Everyone has the capacity to be peacemakers; it is everyone's responsibility. Everyday life peacebuilding as a new approach encapsulates this (see Brewer *et al.*, 2018) and democratises peacebuilding by empowering people to be their own peacebuilders not only those with training and qualifications in conflict resolution. This approach should be expanded to monotheist peacebuilding; it becomes the responsibility of every person of faith in their everyday lives to advance peace. Monotheist peacebuilders should therefore explore the potential of groups that religious practice normally marginalises in order to include them as religious peace-builders where relevant. They should be integral to religious practice generally and to monotheist peacebuilding as well. This again reinforces the point that the peacebuilding contributions of religious women, non-Western peoples, and other hitherto excluded people and groups should be incorporated and celebrated.

My final comment is not as a sociologist of religious peacebuilding but as a person of faith. There are many ways forward for religion and for monotheist peacebuilding. I have only highlighted some. If we follow God's light though, I am sure that the path ahead will be better illuminated.

References

Abu-Nimar, M. (2001) A Framework for Nonviolence and Peacebuilding in Islam. *Journal of Law and Religion* 15, 217–65.

Abu-Nimar, M. (2003) *Nonviolence and Peacebuilding in Islam*. Gainesville: University Press of Florida.

Abu-Nimar, M. (2013) Religion and Peacebuilding. In Mac Ginty, R. ed., *Routledge Handbook of Peacebuilding*. London: Routledge, pp. 69–80.

Abu-Nimar, M. (2022) Religion in Peacebuilding: An Emerging Force for Change. In Mitchell, J., Millar, S., Po, F., and Percy, M. eds., *The Wiley Blackwell Companion to Religion and Peace*. Chichester: Wiley Blackwell, pp. 562–72.

Abu-Nimar, M. and Augsburger, D. (2009) *Peace Building By, Between and Beyond Muslims and Evangelical Christians*. Lanham, MD: Lexington Books.

Abu-Nimar, M., Khoury, A., and Welty, M. (2007) *Unity and Diversity: Inter-Faith Dialogue in the Middle East*. Washington, DC: United States Institute of Peace.

Afrini, M. R. (2019) *Religious Peacebuilding in the Democratic Republic of the Congo*. Brussels: Peter Lang.

Ahmed, M. and Rae, J. D. (2022) Women's Empowerment and Peacebuilding in an Islamic Context. In Mitchell, J., Millar, S., Po, F., and Percy, M. eds., *The Wiley Blackwell Companion to Religion and Peace*. Chichester: Wiley Blackwell, pp. 101–11.

Akenson, D. (1992) *God's People*. Ithaca, NY: Cornell University Press.

Allen, J. (2007) *Rabble-Rouser for Peace*. London: Rider.

Altglass, V. (2014) *From Yoga to Kabbalah*. Oxford: Oxford University Press.

Amstutz, M. (2004) *The Healing of Nations*. Lanham, MD: Rowman and Littlefield.

Anand, D. (2011) *Hindu Nationalism in India and the Politics of Fear*. London: Palgrave.

Anderlini, S. (2007) *Women Building Peace*. Boulder, CO: Lynne Reinner.

Appleby, S. (2000) *The Ambivalence of the Sacred*. Lanham, MD: Rowman and Littlefield.

Appleby, S. (2012) Religious Violence: The Strong, the Weak, and the Pathological. *Practical Matters* 5, 1–25.

Appleby, S. (2015a) Religious Violence: The Strong, Weak and Pathological. In Omer, A., Appleby, S., and Little, D. eds., *The Oxford Handbook of Religion, Conflict and Peacebuilding*. Oxford: Oxford University Press, pp. 33–60.

Appleby, S. (2015b) The New Name for Peace? Religion and Development as Partners in Strategic Peacebuilding. In Omer, A., Appleby, S., and Little, D. eds., *The Oxford Handbook of Religion, Conflict and Peacebuilding*. Oxford: Oxford University Press, pp. 183–211.

Appleby, S. (2022) Ambivalence, Diversity and the Possibility of Religious Peacebuilding. In Mitchell, J., Millar, S., Po, F., and Percy, M. eds., *The Wiley Blackwell Companion to Religion and Peace*. Chichester: Wiley Blackwell, pp. 462–71.

Armstrong, K. (2007) *The Bible: A Biography*. London: Atlantic Books.

Armstrong, K. (2014) *Fields of Blood: Religion and the History of Violence*. London: Vintage.

Arterbon, S. and Fleton, J. (2001) *Toxic Faith*. Colorado Springs, CO: WaterBrook and Multnomah.

Atack, I. (2005) *The Ethics of Peace and War*. Edinburgh: Edinburgh University Press.

Axelrod, A. and Phillips, C. (2004) *Encyclopaedia of Wars*. New York: Facts on File Publishers.

Barnes, I. P. (2005) Was the Northern Irish Conflict Religious? *Journal of Contemporary Religion* 20, 55–69.

Beck, U. (2010) *A God of One's Own*. Cambridge: Polity Press.

Benthall, J. (1997) The Red Cross and Red Crescent Movement and Islamic Societies, with Special Reference to Jordan. *British Journal of Middle Eastern Studies* 24, 157–77.

Bettiza, G. (2019) *Finding Faith in Foreign Policy*. Oxford: Oxford University Press.

Blythe, J. and Gamble, R. (2022) Contemporary Buddhist Peace Movements. In Mitchell, J., Millar, S., Po, F., and Percy, M. eds., *The Wiley Blackwell Companion to Religion and Peace*. Chichester: Wiley Blackwell, pp. 275–88.

Brewer, J. D. (2003) *C Wright Mills and the Ending of Violence*. London: Palgrave.

Brewer, J. D. (2007) Sociology and Theology Reconsidered: Religious Sociology and Sociology of Religion in Britain. *Journal of the History of Human Sciences* 20(2), 7–28.

Brewer, J. D. (2010) *Peace Processes: A Sociological Approach*. Cambridge: Polity Press.

Brewer, J. D. (2013) *The Public Value of the Social Sciences*. London: Bloomsbury Press.

Brewer, J. D. (2015) Northern Ireland: Religion, Religiosity and Politics in a Changing Society. In Hunt, S. ed., *Global Handbook of Contemporary Christianity*. Leiden: Brill, pp. 208–27.

Brewer, J. D. (2019) The Public Value of the Sociology of Religion. In Lindgreen, A., Koenig-Lewis, N., Kitchener, M., et al. eds., *Public Value: Deepening, Enriching and Broadening the Theory and the Practice*. London: Routledge, pp. 222–35.

Brewer, J. D. (2021a) Religious Contributions to Peace in Northern Ireland: The Case of the Redemptorists. In Wijesinghe, S. L. and Silva, R. eds., *Dynamics of Mission: Essays in Honor of Oswald B. Firth*. Colombo: Centre for Religion and Society, pp. 77–92.

Brewer, J. D. (2021b) Religion and Peacebuilding. In Richmond, O. and Visoka, G. eds., *The Oxford Handbook of Peacebuilding, Statebuilding and Peace Formation*. Oxford: Oxford University Press, pp. 520–31.

Brewer, J. D. (2022a) *An Advanced Introduction to the Sociology of Peace Processes*. Cheltenham: Edward Elgar.

Brewer, J. D. (2022b) Sociological Conceptualizations of Religion and Peacebuilding. In Mitchell, J., Millar, S., Po, F., and Percy, M. eds., *The Wiley Blackwell Companion to Religion and Peace*. Chichester: Wiley Blackwell, pp. 497–508.

Brewer, J. D., Hayes, B. C., Teeney, F., et al. (2018) *The Sociology of Everyday Life Peacebuilding*. London: Palgrave.

Brewer, J. D. and Higgins, G. (1998) *Anti-Catholicism in Ireland 1600–1998*. London: Palgrave.

Brewer, J. D. and Higgins, G. (1999) Understanding Anti-Catholicism in Northern Ireland. *Sociology* 33, 235–55.

Brewer, J., Higgins, G., and Teeney, F. (2010) Religious Peacemaking: A Conceptualisation. *Sociology* 44, 1019–37.

Brewer, J. D., Higgins, G. and Teeney, F. (2011) *Religion, Civil Society and Peace in Northern Ireland*. Oxford: Oxford University Press.

Brewer, J. D., Mitchell, D. and Leavey, G. (2013) *Ex-Combatants, Religion and Peace in Northern Ireland*. London: Palgrave.

Brewer, J. D. and Teeney, F. (2015) Religion, Violence, Tolerance and Peace in Northern Ireland. In Brunn, S. ed., *The Changing World Religion Map*. New York: Springer, pp. 3649–68.

Brewer, J. D. and Wahidin, A. (2021) Eds. *Ex-Combatants' Voices*. London: Palgrave.

Brightman, E. S. (1940) *A Philosophy of Religion*. New York: Greenwood Press.

Brudholm, T. and Cushman, T. (2009) Eds. *The Religious in Response to Mass Atrocity*. Cambridge: Cambridge University Press.

Cejka, M. and Bamat, T. (2003) Eds. *Artisans of Peace: Grassroots Peacemaking among Christian Communities*. Maryknoll, NY: Orbis Books.

Chaves, J. (2015) Latin American Liberation Theology. In Hunt, S. ed., *Handbook of Global Christianity*. Leiden: Brill, pp. 113–30.

Clarke, S. (2014) *The Justification of Religious Violence*. Oxford: Wiley Blackwell.

Coward, H. and Smith, G. (2004) Eds. *Religion and Peacebuilding*. New York: State University of New York Press.

Davie, G. (2000) *Religion in Modern Europe*. Oxford: Oxford University Press.

Dawkins, R. (2006) *The God Delusion*. London: Bantam Press.

Dilley, F. (2000) A Finite God Reconsidered. *International Journal of the Philosophy of Religion* 47, 29–41.

Dunlop, J. (1995) *A Precarious Belonging*. Belfast: Blackstaff Press.

Eig, J. (2023) *King: The Life of Martin Luther King*. London: Simon and Schuster.

Eisen, R. (2011) *The Peace and Violence of Judaism*. Oxford: Oxford University Press.

Fair, C. and Patel, P. (2019) Explaining Why Some Muslims Support Islamic Political Violence. *Political Science Quarterly* 134(2), pp. 245–76.

Firestone, R. (1996) Conceptions of Holy War in Biblical and Quranic Tradition. *Journal of Religious Ethics* 21(4), 99–123.

Firestone, R. (2012) *Holy War in Judaism: The Fall and Rise of a Controversial Idea*. Oxford: Oxford University Press.

Fisk, A. and Rai, T. (2015) *Virtuous Violence*. Cambridge: Cambridge University Press.

Freedman, M. (2019) Fighting from the Pulpit: Religious Leaders and Violent Conflict in Israel. *Journal of Conflict Resolution* 63(10), 2262–88.

Ganiel, G. (2008) *Evangelism and Conflict in Northern Ireland*. London: Palgrave.

Ganiel, G. (2019) *Unity Pilgrims: The Life of Fr Gerry Reynolds CSsR*. Dublin: Redemptorist Communications.

Ganiel, G. (2021) Protestants and Peacebuilding. In Coquelin, O., Bastiat, B., and Healy, F. eds., *Northern Ireland*. Brussels: Peter Lang, pp. 97–116.

Ganiel, G. and Yohannis, J. (2019) *Considering Grace: Presbyterians and the Troubles*. Dublin: Merrion Press.

Ganiel, G. and Yohannis, J. (2022) Presbyterians, Forgiveness and Dealing with the Past in Northern Ireland. *Religions* 13(1), 41, at https://doi.org/10.3390/rel13010041.

Garrigan, S. (2010) *The Real Peace Process*. London: Equinox.

Gentile, E. (2006) *Politics as Religion*. Princeton, NJ: Princeton University Press.

Gentile, E. and Mallett, R. (2000) The Sacralisation of Politics. *Totalitarian Movements and Political Religions* 1(1), 18–55.

Ghannoushi, S. (2011) The Propagation of Neo-Orientalism. *Al Jazeera*, 27 January, www.ljazeera.com/indepth/opinion/20112611591745716.html.

Gopin, M. (1994) Is There a Jewish God of Peace? In Polner, M. and Goodman, N. eds., *The Challenge of Shalom*. Philadelphia, PA: New Society, pp. 32–9.

Gopin, M. (2000) *Between Eden and Armageddon: The Future of World Religions, Violence and Peacemaking*. Oxford: Oxford University Press.

Gopin, M. (2002) *Holy War, Holy Peace: How Religion Can Bring Peace to the Middle East*. Oxford: Oxford University Press.

Gopin, M. (2003) Judaism and Peacebuilding in the Context of Middle East Conflict. In Johnston, D. ed., *Faith Based Diplomacy*. Oxford: Oxford University Press, pp. 106–18.

Gopin, M. (2004) Judaism and Peacebuilding. In Coward, H. and Smith, G. eds., *Religion and Peacebuilding*. New York: State University of New York Press, pp. 111–28.

Gopin, M. (2009) *To Make the Earth Whole: The Art of Citizen Diplomacy in an Age of Religious Militancy*. Lanham, MD: Rowman and Littlefield.

Gopin, M. (2012) *Bridges across an Impossible Divide*. Oxford: Oxford University Press.

Gopin, M. (2015) Negotiating Secular and Religious Contributions to Social Change and Peacebuilding. In Omer, A., Appleby, S., and Little, D. eds., *The Oxford Handbook of Religion, Conflict and Peacebuilding*. Oxford: Oxford University Press, pp. 355–79.

Gopin, M. (2016) *Healing the Heart of Conflict*. Scotts Valley, CA: CreateSpace Independent Publishing Platform.

Gopin, M. (2017) *Compassionate Judaism*. Scotts Valley, CA: CreateSpace Independent Publishing Platform.

Gopin, M. (2022) *Compassionate Reasoning: Changing the Mind to Change the World*. Oxford: Oxford University Press.

Gorski, P., Perry, S., and Tisby, J. (2022) *The Flag and the Cross*. Oxford: Oxford University Press.

Griffin, D. R. (1991) *God, Power and Evil*. Lanham, MD: University Press of America.

Griffin, D. R. and Cobb, J. B. (1976) *Process Theology*. Philadelphia, PA: Westminster Press.

Hadley, M. (2001) *The Spiritual Roots of Restorative Justice*. Albany: State University of New York Press.

Hayes, J. D. (1952) *A Study of the Finite God of Edgar Sheffield Brightman*. Loyola University MA Thesis. Paper 1040. http://ecommons.luc.edu/luc_theses/1040.

Haynes, J. (2009) Conflict, Conflict Resolution and Peacebuilding: The Role of Religion in Mozambique, Nigeria and Cambodia. *Commonwealth and Comparative Politics* 47(1), 52–75.

Haynes, J. (2022) International Relations, Religion and Peace. In Mitchell, J., Millar, S., Po, F., and Percy, M. eds., *The Wiley Blackwell Companion to Religion and Peace*. Chichester: Wiley Blackwell, pp. 475–84.

Hayward, S. (2015) Women, Religion and Peacebuilding. In Omer, A., Appleby, S., and Little, D. eds., *The Oxford Handbook of Religion, Conflict and Peacebuilding*. Oxford: Oxford University Press, pp. 307–32.

Hayward, S. and Marshall, K. (2015) Eds. *Women, Religion and Peacebuilding: Illuminating the Unseen*. Washington, DC: United States Institute of Peace Press.

Heelas, P. (1996) *The New Age Movement*. Oxford: Blackwell.

Heelas, P. and Woodhead, L. (2004) *The Spiritual Revolution*. Oxford: Wiley Blackwell.

Hoover, D. and Johnston, D. (2012) Eds. *Religion and Foreign Affairs*. Waco, TX: Baylor University Press.

Hughes, M. (2008) *Methodism, Peace and War in the Twentieth Century*. Norwich: Methodist.

Ignatieff, M. (2017) *The Ordinary Virtues*. London: Harvard University Press.

Isaacs, M. (2016) Sacred Violence or Strategic Faith? Disentangling the Relationship between Religion and Violence in Armed Conflict. *Journal of Peace Research* 53(2), 211–25.

Jakelić, S. (2015) Secular-Religious Encounters in Peacebuilding. In Omer, A., Appleby, S., and Little, D. eds., *The Oxford Handbook of Religion, Conflict and Peacebuilding*. Oxford: Oxford University Press, pp. 124–45.

Jerryson, M., Juergensmeyer, M., and Kitts, M. (2013) Eds. *Oxford Handbook of Religion and Violence*. Oxford: Oxford University Press.

Johns, J. (1992) Christianity and Islam. In McManners, J. ed., *The Oxford Illustrated History of Christianity*. Oxford: Oxford University Press, pp. 163–95.

Johnston, D. (2003) *Faith-Based Diplomacy*. Oxford: Oxford University Press.

Johnston, D. (2011) *Religion, Terror and Error*. Santa Barbara, CA: Praeger Publications.

Johnston, D. and Sampson, C. (1994) Eds. *Religion: The Missing Dimension in Statecraft*. Oxford: Oxford University Press.

Jones, D. M. and Smith, M. L. R. (2014) *Sacred Violence*. London: Palgrave.

Juergensmeyer, M. (2000) *Terror in the Mind of God*. Berkeley, CA: University of California Press.

Kadayifci-Orellana, S. A. (2015) Peacebuilding in the Muslim World. In Omer, A., Appleby, S., and Little, D. eds., *The Oxford Handbook of Religion, Conflict and Peacebuilding*. Oxford: Oxford University Press, pp. 430–69.

Kaldor, M. (1999) *New and Old Wars*. Cambridge: Polity Press.

Karem, A. (2022) Genocide Prevention, Religion and Development. In Mitchell, J., Millar, S., Po, F., and Percy, M. eds., *The Wiley Blackwell Companion to Religion and Peace*. Chichester: Wiley Blackwell, pp. 530–40.

Kelly, G. (2021) Reconciliation and Peacebuilding. In Richmond, O. and Visoka, G. eds., *The Oxford Handbook of Peacebuilding, Statebuilding and Peace Formation*. Oxford: Oxford University Press, pp. 506–19.

King, A. (2022) Hinduism: The Culture of Peace and the Ethics of War. In Mitchell, J., Millar, S., Po, F., and Percy, M. eds., *The Wiley Blackwell Companion to Religion and Peace*. Chichester: Wiley Blackwell, pp. 197–2015.

Kirby, D. (2021) Religious Women and the Northern Ireland Troubles. *Journal of Religious History* 45(3), 412–34.

Kurtz, L. R. and Smithey, L. (2018) Eds. *The Paradox of Repression and Nonviolent Movements*. Syracuse, NY: Syracuse University Press.

Lederach, J. P. (1995) *Preparing for Peace*. Syracuse, NY: Syracuse University Press.

Lederach, J. P. (1997) *Building Peace*. Washington, DC: United States Institute of Peace Press.

Lederach, J. P. (1999a) Justpeace: The Challenge of the 21st Century. In van Tongeren, P. ed., *People Building Peace*. Utrecht: European Centre for Conflict Prevention, pp. 27–36.

Lederach, J. P. (1999b) *The Journey toward Reconciliation*. Harrisonburg, VA: Herald Press.

Lederach, J. P. (2002) *A Handbook of International Peacebuilding*. Indianapolis, IN: Jossey-Bass.

Lederach, J. P. (2005) *The Moral Imagination*. Oxford: Oxford University Press.

Lederach, J. P. (2014) *Reconcile*. Harrisonburg, VA: Herald Press.

Lederach, J. P. (2015) Spirituality and Religious Peacebuilding. In Omer, A., Appleby, S., and Little, D. eds., *The Oxford Handbook of Religion, Conflict and Peacebuilding*. Oxford: Oxford University Press, pp. 541–68.

Lederach, J. P. (2022) Peacebuilding and Religion. In Mitchell, J., Millar, S., Po, F., and Percy, M. eds., *The Wiley Blackwell Companion to Religion and Peace*. Chichester: Wiley Blackwell, pp. 63–78.

Leichty, J. and Clegg, C. (2001) *Moving Beyond Sectarianism*. Dublin: Columba.

Leiden, K. (2021) The Ethics of Liberal Peacebuilding. In Richmond, O. and Visoka, G. eds., *The Oxford Handbook of Peacebuilding, Statebuilding and Peace Formation*. Oxford: Oxford University Press, pp. 42–58.

Little, D. (2007) *Peacemakers in Action*. Cambridge: Cambridge University Press.

LiVecche, M. and Biggar, N. (2022) Just War, Critique and Conscientious Objection. In Mitchell, J., Millar, S., Po, F., and Percy, M. eds., *The Wiley Blackwell Companion to Religion and Peace*. Chichester: Wiley Blackwell, pp. 405–16.

Love, M. C. (2022) Just Peace: From Versailles to Today. In Mitchell, J., Millar, S., Po, F., and Percy, M. eds., *The Wiley Blackwell Companion to Religion and Peace*. Chichester: Wiley Blackwell, pp. 417–27.

Mac Ginty, R. and Richmond, O. (2013) The Local Turn in Peace Building: A Critical Agenda for Peace. *Third World Quarterly* 34(5), 763–83.

Mamdani, M. (2002) Good Muslims, Bad Muslims: A Political Perspective on Culture and Terrorism. *American Anthropologist* 104(3), 766–75.

Margalit, A. (2010) *On Compromise and Rotten Compromises*. Princeton, NJ: Princeton University Press.

Markham, I. (2022) Relationships between Religion and Peace. In Mitchell, J., Millar, S., Po, F., and Percy, M. eds., *The Wiley Blackwell Companion to Religion and Peace*. Chichester: Wiley Blackwell, pp. 39–48.

McCarthy, E. S. (2022) Religious Warrants: Virtue, Nonviolence and Just Peace. In Mitchell, J., Millar, S., Po, F., and Percy, M. eds., *The Wiley Blackwell Companion to Religion and Peace*. Chichester: Wiley Blackwell, pp. 428–37.

McKay, S. (2000) *Northern Protestants: An Unsettled People*. Belfast: Blackstaff Press.

McKeever, M. (2017) *One Man, One God: The Peace Ministry of Fr Alec Reid*. Dublin: Redemptorist Communications.

Mitchell, C. (2006) The Religious Content of Ethnic Identities. *Sociology* 40, 1135–52.

Mitchell, J., King, A., Haywood, S., et al. (2022) World Religions and Peace. In Mitchell, J., Millar, S., Po, F., and Percy, M. eds., *The Wiley Blackwell Companion to Religion and Peace*. Chichester: Wiley Blackwell, pp. 21–38.

Mitchell, J., Millar, S., Po, F., and Percy, M. (2022) Eds. *The Wiley Blackwell Companion to Religion and Peace*. Chichester: Wiley Blackwell.

Mitchell, J. and Ray, J. (2021) *War and Religion: A Very Short Introduction*. Oxford: Oxford University Press.

Morrow, W. (1998) Toxic Religion and the Daughters of Job. *Studies in Religion* 27(3), 263–76.

Murphy, A. (2011) Ed. *The Blackwell Companion to Religion and Violence*. Oxford: Blackwell.

Ngo, T., Yu, D. S., and Van Der Veer, P. (2015) Religion and Peace in Asia. In Omer, A., Appleby, S., and Little, D. eds., *The Oxford Handbook of Religion, Conflict and Peacebuilding*. Oxford: Oxford University Press, pp. 407–29.

Nicosia, P. S. (2017) Faith-Based Peacebuilding: Insights from the Three Main Monotheisms. *Athens Journal of Social Science* 4(1), 7–24.

Ochs, P. (2015) The Possibility and Limits of Interreligious Dialogue. In Omer, A., Appleby, S., and Little, D. eds., *The Oxford Handbook of Religion, Conflict and Peacebuilding*. Oxford: Oxford University Press, pp. 488–515.

Omer, A. (2020) *Decolonizing Religion and Peacebuilding*. Oxford: Oxford University Press.

Omer, A., Appleby, S., and Little, D. (2015) Eds. *The Oxford Handbook of Religion, Conflict and Peacebuilding*. Oxford: Oxford University Press.

Orsi, R. (2022) The Study of Religion on the Other Side of the Good Religion/ Bad Religion Binary. *Journal of Religious Ethics* 50(2), 312–17.

Philpott, D. (2006) *The Politics of Past Evil*. Notre Dame, IN: University of Notre Dame Press.

Philpott, D. (2007a) What Religion Brings to Restorative Justice. *Journal of International Affairs* 61, 93–110.

Philpott, D. (2007b) Explaining the Political Ambivalence of Religion. *American Political Science Review* 103, 516–28.

Philpott, D. (2009) When Faith Meets History: The Influence of Religion in Transitional Justice. In Brudholm, T. and Cushman, T. eds. *The Religious in Response to Mass Atrocity*. Cambridge: Cambridge University Press, pp. 174–212.

Philpott, D. (2012) *Just and Unjust Peace*. Oxford: Oxford University Press.

Philpott, D. (2015) Reconciliation, Politics and Transitional Justice. In Omer, A., Appleby, S., and Little, D. eds., *The Oxford Handbook of Religion, Conflict and Peacebuilding*. Oxford: Oxford University Press, pp. 335–54.

Power, M. (2007) *From Ecumenism to Community Relations*. Dublin: Irish Academic Press.

Richmond, O. and Mac Ginty, R. (2014) Where Now for the Critique of the Liberal Peace? *Cooperation and Conflict* 50(2), 171–89.

Rios, S. (2015) *Religion, Social Memory and Conflict*. London: Palgrave.

Ruane, J. and Todd, J. (1996) *The Dynamics of Conflict in Northern Ireland*. Cambridge: Cambridge University Press.

Sadeghi-Boroujerdi, E. (2023) Iran's Uprisings for 'Women, Life, Freedom'. *Politics*, published online first 23 March at https://doi.org/10.1177/02633957 2311159351.

Sampson, C. and Lederach, J. P. (2000) Eds. *From the Ground Up: Mennonite Contributions to International Peacebuilding.* Oxford: Oxford University Press.

Sandal, N. (2022) Religious Leaders and Peace. In Mitchell, J., Millar, S., Po, F., and Percy, M. eds., *The Wiley Blackwell Companion to Religion and Peace.* Chichester: Wiley Blackwell, pp. 552–61.

Schlack, A. (2009) *The Role of Religion in Peacebuilding and Conflict Resolution.* Saarbrucken: Verlag Dr Muller (VDM).

Schreiter, R., Appleby, S., and Powers, G. (2010) Eds. *Peacebuilding: Catholic Theology, Ethics and Praxis.* Maryknoll, NY: Orbis Books.

Scull, M. (2023) The Northern Ireland Reconciliation Bill Highlights the Complicated Role of Catholic Church during the Troubles. *The Conversation,* 4 January, Accessible online at https://theconversation.com/northern-ireland-reconciliation-bill-highlights-complicated-role-of-catholic-church-during-the-troubles).

Segell, G. (2023) An Alternative View of the Israel-Palestine Dispute: The Eschatological Dimension. *Journal of the Centre of Middle Eastern Studies* 16(1), 1–11.

Shore, M. (2009) *Religion and Conflict Resolution.* Farnham: Ashgate.

Shriver, D. (1998) *An Ethic for Enemies.* Oxford: Oxford University Press.

Smithey, L. (2011) *Unionists, Loyalists, and Conflict Transformation in Northern Ireland.* Oxford: Oxford University Press.

Smock. D. (2001) *Faith Based NGOs and International Peacebuilding.* Washington, DC: United States Institute of Peace Press.

Smock, D. (2002) *Interfaith Dialogue and Peacebuilding.* Washington, DC: United States Institute of Peace Press.

Smock, D. (2006) *Religious Contributions to Peacemaking.* Washington, DC: United States Institute of Peace Press.

Smock, D. (2008) *Religion in World Affairs.* Washington, DC: United States Institute of Peace Press.

Steen-Johnsen, T. (2017) *State and Politics in Religious Peacebuilding.* London: Palgrave.

Tabaar, M. A., Huang, R., Chandra, K., et al. (2023) How Religious Are 'Religious' Conflicts? *International Studies Review* 25(3), 1–30. published first online at https://doi.org/10.1093/isr/viad027.

Taliep, N., Lazarus, S., Seedat, M., and Cochrane, J. (2016) The Role of Religious Leaders in Anti-apartheid Mobilisation. *Religion, State and Society* 44(4), 331–48.

Tarusarira, J. (2015) Christianity, Resistance and Conflict Resolution in Zimbabwe. In Hunt, S. ed., *Handbook of Global Christianity.* Leiden: Brill, pp. 266–84.

Torrance, A. (2006) *The Theological Grounds for Advocating Forgiveness in the Sociopolitical Realm*. Belfast: Centre for Contemporary Christianity.

Turner, C. (2021) Transitional Justice and Peacebuilding. In Richmond, O. and Visoka, G. eds., *The Oxford Handbook of Peacebuilding, Statebuilding and Peace Formation*. Oxford: Oxford University Press, pp. 488–505.

Twiss, S., Simon, M. G., and Petersen, R. (2015) Eds. *Religion and Public Policy*. Cambridge: Cambridge University Press.

Valentine, L. (2013) Quakers, War and Peacemaking. In Angell, S. and Dandelion, B. P. eds., *Oxford Handbook of Quaker Studies*. Oxford: Oxford University Press, pp. 363–76.

Vencatsamy, B. (2024) The World Religions Paradigm: Why Context Matters in Religious Studies. *Critical Research in Religion* 12(1), 12–25.

Volf, M. (1996) *Exclusion and Embrace*. Nashville, TN: Abingdon Press.

Volf, M. (2006) *The End of Memory*. Grand Rapids, MI: Eerdmans.

Wadud, A. (2006) *Inside the Gender Jihad*. Oxford: Oxford University Press.

Walsham, A. (2006) *Charitable Hatred*. Manchester: Manchester University Press.

Wells, R. (2004) *Friendship toward Peace*. Dublin: Columba Press.

White, M. (2011) *The Great Big Book of Horrible Things*. New York: W.W. Norton.

Whitnall, C. (2022) In the Presence of Whose Enemies? *Journal of the Centre for the Study of Bible and Violence* 1(1), 6–42.

Wijesignhe, S. L. and Brewer, J. D. (2018) Peace Religiosity and Forgiveness among War Victims in Sri Lanka. In Brewer, J. D., Hayes, B. C., and Teeney, F. eds., *The Sociology of Compromise after Conflict*. London: Palgrave, pp. 129–55.

Wijesignhe, S. L. and Silva, R. (2021) Eds. *Dynamics of Mission: Essays in Honor of Oswald B. Firth OMI*. Colombo: Centre for Religion and Society.

Wolterstorff, N. (1983) *Until Justice and Peace Embrace*. Grand Rapids, MI: Eerdmans.

Wolterstorff, N. (2008) *Justice, Rights and Wrongs*. Princeton, NJ: Princeton University Press.

Wolterstorff, N. (2013) *Journey toward Justice*. Ada, MI: Baker Academic.

Wolterstorff, N. (2015) *Justice in Love*. Grand Rapids, MI: Eerdmans.

Yazdani, A. (2020) The Culture of Peace and Religious Tolerance from an Islamic Perspective. *Veritas* 47, published online at http://dx.doi.org/10.4067/SO18-927320200000300151.

Cambridge Elements ☰

Religion and Monotheism

Paul K. Moser
Loyola University Chicago

Paul K. Moser is Professor of Philosophy at Loyola University Chicago. He is the author of *God in Moral Experience; Paul's Gospel of Divine Self-Sacrifice; The Divine Goodness of Jesus; Divine Guidance; Understanding Religious Experience; The God Relationship; The Elusive God* (winner of national book award from the Jesuit Honor Society); *The Evidence for God; The Severity of God; Knowledge and Evidence* (all Cambridge University Press); and *Philosophy after Objectivity* (Oxford University Press); coauthor of *Theory of Knowledge* (Oxford University Press); editor of *Jesus and Philosophy* (Cambridge University Press) and *The Oxford Handbook of Epistemology* (Oxford University Press); and coeditor of *The Wisdom of the Christian Faith* (Cambridge University Press). He is the coeditor with Chad Meister of the book series *Cambridge Studies in Religion, Philosophy, and Society.*

Chad Meister
Affiliate Scholar, Ansari Institute for Global Engagement with Religion, University of Notre Dame

Chad Meister is Affiliate Scholar at the Ansari Institute for Global Engagement with Religion at the University of Notre Dame. His authored and co-authored books include *Evil: A Guide for the Perplexed* (Bloomsbury Academic, 2nd edition); *Introducing Philosophy of Religion* (Routledge); *Introducing Christian Thought* (Routledge, 2nd edition); and *Contemporary Philosophical Theology* (Routledge). He has edited or co-edited the following: *The Oxford Handbook of Religious Diversity* (Oxford University Press); *Debating Christian Theism* (Oxford University Press); with Paul Moser, *The Cambridge Companion to the Problem of Evil* (Cambridge University Press); and with Charles Taliaferro, *The History of Evil* (Routledge, in six volumes). He is the co-editor with Paul Moser of the book series *Cambridge Studies in Religion, Philosophy, and Society.*

About the Series

This Cambridge Element series publishes original concise volumes on monotheism and its significance. Monotheism has occupied inquirers since the time of the Biblical patriarch, and it continues to attract interdisciplinary academic work today. Engaging, current, and concise, the Elements benefit teachers, researched, and advanced students in religious studies, Biblical studies, theology, philosophy of religion, and related fields.

Cambridge Elements ≡

Religion and Monotheism

Elements in the Series

A full series listing is available at: www.cambridge.org/er&m

Printed in the United States
by Baker & Taylor Publisher Services